THE BEAR MARKET SURVIVAL GUIDE

The Bear Market Survival Guide

Timothy J. McIntosh

Writers Club Press

New York Lincoln Shanghai

The Bear Market Survival Guide

Writers Club Press
an imprint of iUniverse, Inc.

iUniverse books may be ordered through booksellers or by contacting:

iUniverse
2021 Pine Lake Road, Suite 100
Lincoln, NE 68512
www.iuniverse.com
1-800-Authors (1-800-288-4677)

ISBN-13: 978-0-595-27224-2 (pbk)
ISBN-13: 978-0-595-65660-8 (cloth)
ISBN-10: 0-595-27224-X (pbk)
ISBN-10: 0-595-65660-9 (cloth)

Printed in the United States of America

Acknowledgments

I wish to first thank my family; wife Kim and sons Beckett and Emerson for giving me the time for this endeavor. I would also like to thank my Father, Tom, for his helpful reviews. Dad passed away in 2004. He will always be in my thoughts. To Leah Cassora, thanks for providing astute editing of this second edition. Additional gratitude is due to my business partners Paul MacNamara, Margaret Coughtrie, and Mark Laisure for allowing me time to play author.

To all the academics, analysts, and investment managers that have published research utilized in this book, I am extremely grateful. This book relies heavily on the academic research published primarily in the past ten years. It was indispensable to supporting the primary arguments of this book.

Introduction

Investing, I believe, is much like tennis. My goal while playing tennis is to keep the ball in play and make the fewest errors possible. I let the other player make the critical mistakes. These mistakes add up and, by the end are too much to overcome. The match is mine. Investing is the same game. My goal as an investment manager is to not make big mistakes. Big mistakes result in big losses and unhappy clients. By simply keeping investment losses to a respectable amount, I believe I can generate significant long-term returns for my clients. Many investors believe that garnering excellent returns can only be earned in big up years. That is hardly the case. A prudent investor should know that "striking it rich" in the stock market is only for the gambler. And the fact is most gamblers lose their shirt.

This book's maxim, therefore, is about avoiding the major blunder of investing; getting mauled during a bear stock market. Bear stock markets are ugly and nasty and occur every couple of years. They take no prisoners. A bear market can wipe out ten years of solid investment returns in less than six months. We have just witnessed the worst bear stock market since the Depression in the 1930's.

Fortunately, I have developed an investment strategy that minimizes the impact of bear markets. It is a time-tested approach that has minimized the impact of every bear market over the past 28 years. More importantly, the long-term returns of this defensive strategy are superlative. Now, you won't learn how to become a millionaire overnight here. But you will find out how to build a portfolio good enough to retire on time, send those kids to college, or simply have a little more fun.

I begin in Chapter 1 with a description of bear stock markets. I discuss the major bear markets over the past fifty years. You will learn what the average bear market looks like and, more importantly how one can impact an investment portfolio. In Chapter 2, I give a review of recent academic studies on correlation. Don't panic; it is easier than you think. Correlation is simply how two assets move together. I'll also discuss how investing internationally does not offer the same benefits as it once did.

Chapter 3 presents my sector strategy. I present evidence on how sector investing has changed. Most importantly, I list which sectors have been the best performers over the last twenty-eight years. Chapter 4 discusses my framework for investing. I'll discuss how your investments should be assembled, and how many stocks you should have in your portfolio. Chapters 5, 6, 7, and 8 present my recommended sectors. These are the sectors of the economy you should focus your investment dollars in. Each of these four chapters reviews the sector in detail including future prospects, breakdown of major companies, and rules of individual selection.

Chapter 9 features the income-producing investments I recommend to balance your portfolio. One of the most important topics, fundamental analysis, is explained in Chapter 10. You will learn some basic tools to dissect a balance sheet and income statement. Chapter 11 displays my buy and sell process for individual stock selection. This chapter will give you my insights into Wall Street and how to take advantage of sector rotation. I present five case studies to help you better understand my investment process. Chapter 12 examines small-cap companies. I present evidence that small company stocks are highly overrated and offer investors minimal benefits.

Chapter 13 examines mutual funds and ETFs. I have added this chapter for those investors who are either beginners or do not have the time to select individual stocks. My defensive strategy can still be followed through proper use of professionally managed investment funds. Finally, Chapter 14 sums everything up and offers several model portfolios. Each portfolio is back-tested over the past twenty-eight years. Here is where all the research and theory come together. I will show you how each model portfolio can get you through the worst of bear markets while still offering compelling investment returns.

My recommended sectors and model portfolios will look quite different from a financial plan you would see from a typical financial planner or investment magazine. My recommendations look different for a reason; most financial plans written today are simply outdated. I believe they don't work in today's investment climate. In the next fourteen chapters, I'll prove a new investment strategy is necessary to survive and flourish in the 21st century.

Contents

1

Defense Wins

"Wealth is better than poverty, if only for financial reasons,"
— *Woody Allen*

When it comes to the investment book writing business, a few years can be an eternity. If I wrote a book five years ago that slammed the crop of "get rich quick" books permeating the publishing landscape, I might well have been tarred and feathered and ridden out of town on a rail. A top-of-the-line, customized solid gold rail sold on E-Bay for a song.

After all, millions of investors made substantial amounts of money buying technology stocks such as Amazon, Cisco Systems, and Qualcomm during the late 1990s—and lost it all. In fact, featured in a Money Magazine article in March 2000 were three investors who actually did strike it rich. They rode their Qualcomm stock investments during 1999 to a magical 2,619 percent return. One investor had a windfall of $17 million as Qualcomm rose to an astounding $740 a share. It was truly a gilded age on Wall Street. Traders stared at their screens in disbelief and watched the price of dot.com shares skyrocket. Meanwhile, the stocks of companies like Proctor & Gamble or General Electric—dismissed as "brick and mortar dinosaurs" by investors—failed to ignite investor interest even though they made products people actually wanted and used.

Few people, with the exception of market veterans like Warren Buffet and John Bogel, were saying the good times couldn't last. They didn't, and the technology boom went bust in early 2000. By the end of 2001, high-flying Qualcomm stock had fallen over 80 percent in price—down to the price of a AM radio—as investors lost millions. Maybe those investors profiled in Money Magazine cashed out their chips before the impending fall. Maybe not. Most likely not, as opportunities like a Qualcomm are fleeting and dangerous. For every person who did get rich on Qualcomm, 100 others lost their shirts. In effect, putting money in a Qualcomm is no better than going to the casino and betting on whether little silver balls that spin around will land on black or red slots

Despite all the negative fallout from the Go-Go Ninety's, it's not like the era had a monopoly on greed and rose-colored glasses. In fact, there are several examples of inflated markets throughout history. During the nifty-fifty era of 1972, for example, many stocks defied gravity as well. In the early 1970s, a group of companies emerged—called the "nifty fifty"—and quickly became as overvalued as your garden variety, high-flying Internet stock. The nifty fifty's sizzling stock performance and potential to dominate the economy rendered them "must own" stocks by institutional and individual investors alike. In a fashion not so dissimilar from the recent technology bust, large divergences opened up within the stock market. The broad stock market peaked early in 1972, while the amazing nifty fifty stocks established new highs.

It was an era of "who's who" among stocks. The nifty fifty group of 1974 included technology leaders like Xerox, IBM, and Texas Instruments; pharmaceutical companies such as Merck and American Home Products; retail trendsetters like Kmart and J.C. Penney; and consumer product stars Avon, McDonalds, Kodak, and Polaroid. The tongue-in-cheek joke among professional investors at the time was that IBM stood for "I Buy Money", since the prospects for its stock, and its potential impact on the economy, appeared to be a "sure thing".

The 1970s even had its own Qualcomm; Polaroid Corp., a technology darling that traded with a price-earnings ratio above 95 in 1972. A price/earnings ratio of 95 means Polaroid Corp. traded at 95 times a dollars worth of earnings. Polaroid reached a split-adjusted high of $74.56 in May of that year. A little over two years later, it had lost 90 percent of its value. Sure, the stock rebounded, but it never regained the 1972 high. Today, the company plods through bankruptcy court, and trades for pennies a share.

WHAT IS A BEAR MARKET?

In the bad-old days of the 1970s on Wall Street, the nifty-fifty went through what is known as a bear market. Basically, a bear market is defined as a 20 percent drop from the market high. Losing money is never pleasant, and in bear markets, it somehow always feels worse than it is. That's because we hate our losers more than we love our winners. Psychologists say it's one thing to buy a new car. But to have that new car stolen from you, that's a Corvette of a different color. The numbers back that sentiment as behavioral-psychology studies show that stock-market losses tend to hurt three times as much as equivalent gains. Consequently, bear markets usually last for an extended time and take a heavy psychological toll on investors.

It's not like bear markets are as rare as Ivy League professors at a NASCAR race. In fact, the Standard & Poor's 500 stock index has experienced ten bear markets since 1956 (table 1.1). These bear markets have lasted from three months to almost three years, with an average length of 12 months each. The range of declines was steep at 19.9 percent to 48.2 percent, with an average decline of 28.3 percent. After each bear market, it took from 2.3 months to 69.4 months to return to previous highs, with an average recovery period of 18.5 months. The most recent bear market of 2000-2002 lasted 31 months and was the second worst since 1974. Even as I write today, the S&P 500 stock index is still 25 percent below its peak of 1580.

PAST STOCK BEAR MARKETS
S&P 500 Stock Index *

	Decline	Duration	Recovery
	(%)	(months)	(months)
March 2000 to October 2002	48.1	31.2	?
July 1990 to October 1990	19.9	2.9	4.3
Aug. 1987 to Dec. 1987	33.5	3.3	19.7
Jan. 1981 to Aug. 1982	25.8	19.2	2.3
Sept. 1976 to March 1978	19.7	17.5	17.3
Jan. 1973 to October 1974	48.2	20.7	69.4
Nov. 1968 to May 1970	36.1	17.9	21.3
Feb. 1966 to October 1966	22.2	7.9	6.9
Dec. 1961 to June 1962	28.1	6.4	14.3
Aug. 1956 to October 1957	21.6	14.7	11.1

* *Table 1.1, Source: Bloomberg, L.P.; Bernstein 1956-2005*

Notice the highly unusual period between the bear markets of 1990 and 2000-2002. During the 1990s, the U.S. stock market's annual return was 18.2 percent, far above the long-term historical average of 10.8 percent. By the end of the 1990s, the market had not suffered a severe or prolonged period of falling stock prices for a record 10 years. Of course, the long delay between the bear markets only prolonged the damage. But, bear markets generally occur more often. One normally takes place once every five years. Some bear markets can be very painful, especially when the stock market is chock full of speculation. The 1973 and 2001 bear markets are perfect examples of what can take place after rampant speculation. Both markets saw back-to-back stock declines after years of double-digit market gains.

After the speculation is wrung out, it usually takes several years for the market to change direction. Remarkably, after the bear market of

1974, it would take another 8 years for the Dow Jones Industrial Average (DJIA) to recover, finally reaching the 1000 watermark (the 1972 high) in 1982. In the course of ten years, all positive feelings about the stock market had vanished. By 1979, approximately 70 percent of all mutual funds had vanished from existence. That same year, the infamous "Death of Equities" cover appeared in Newsweek.

Bear markets aren't limited to stocks. Bear markets also strike bonds. The most recent bear market in bonds started in December 1998 and continued into January 2000, when surging interest rates sent bond prices (as measured by the 10-year U.S. Treasury bond) tumbling almost 20 percent. Bond prices and interest rates are inversely related: As interest rates rise, bond prices fall, and vice versa. Many factors affect interest rates, including Federal Reserve policy, inflation rates, economic growth, and—importantly—investors' expectations regarding these factors and others. Many times price fluctuations in the bond market can be every bit as frightening as those in the stock market.

BEAR MARKET LESSONS

The real value of a bear market may be what we learn, or re-learn, when one transpires. Here are four important lessons that a bear market brings:

Lesson #1—Diversification really matters. It was easy during the market's bull run of the late 1990s to dismiss the idea that diversification made a difference. Those who put all their eggs into high-risk stock investments learned this lesson first hand. A portfolio that featured a mix of different U.S. stocks and a few bonds didn't avoid a loss, but the diversified approach clearly cushioned the blow.

Lesson #2—Fundamentals make a difference. Until the early months of 2000, speculation was running rampant as to whether the fundamental factors that tend to drive stock markets no longer applied. Had the technological revolution changed the stock market? Could stocks justifiably reach excessive price levels without having sufficient (or even any) profits to back them up? The resounding answer of the past year is an unqualified no. The fundamental financial factors of a company, such as profits and revenue growth, still drive the ultimate price of a stock.

Lesson #3—It's important to maintain a long-term view, even through bear markets. Many investors panicked towards the end of the bear market and sold out their stock positions. Thus, investors rode the bear market to the end, but then jumped off. They never got the opportunity to participate in the eventual recovery. For the twelve months following the end of the recent bear market (October 2002), the S&P 500 stock index gained 32 percent.

If you have an extensive time to let your money grow, what really matters is the next ten, twenty or thirty years. Excessive fluctuations in the markets are a natural occurrence. Don't let excessive fear force you to sell at a stock market bottom. Over time, stock investment values have, on an historical basis, provided the best investment return of all the major asset classes. So if history is any guide, chances are you'll be better off ten, twenty or thirty years from now than you are today.

Lesson #4—The most critical lesson of all is bear markets will happen and can be devastating to your portfolio if ignored. So prepare for the worst. You should expect a bear market once every five years and maintain an investment strategy that contains a defensive plan. If an investor can successfully protect most of their portfolio during a bear market, long-term investment results will be superlative. As any football coach worth his salt will tell you, defense isn't easy. Protecting capital is a tough challenge, especially in a bear market. And attempting to predict when these declines will take place is impossible. So each investor must devise a strategy to make it through these declines with the least amount of damage to a portfolio.

Let's run through an example of how a large loss can affect a portfolio. Joe is your typical investor with most of his money is tied up in stock mutual funds. Joe pays scant attention to risk. His goal is to maximize his return so that he may retire early. Let's assume that Joe has saved up $100,000 over the past several years. If Joe loses 30 percent in a bear stock market, his portfolio shrinks to $70,000. The next year, Joe's funds rebound, gaining back an impressive 30 percent. Is Joe even at this point? Actually, no. Unfortunately, a 30 percent gain only brought poor Joe's portfolio back up to $91,000. Joe actually needs another 9.8 percent to get back to his original $100,000 portfolio. His conundrum is due to the mathematics of investing. Once a portfolio drops in value, its takes an increasing positive return just to get back to even. This is not just a hypothetical event. Many investors learned this mathematics lesson first hand in the current bear stock market.

If Joe wanted to calculate an average return for the two years, he would normally (as most mutual funds do) calculate what is known as an arithmetic average. Arithmetic math simply adds the two returns (30 percent gain, 30 percent loss) and divides by 2. A 30 percent gain in year 1 and a 30 percent loss in year 2 result in a 0 average, divided by 2, still equals 0. However, if Joe really had a 0 percent return, he would still have the original $100,000 investment. Joe does not, he only has $91,000 at this point. This math illustration shows the fault with arithmetic math. It can give an investor misleading information.

Geometric math, on the other hand, is a strict wealth measure. It actually calculates the dollar return for Joe. His geometric return for the two year period is–9.0 percent. This makes complete sense because Joe now has $91,000 left. Geometric math demonstrates the true picture for Joe. The goal of this exercise is not to give you a math lesson, as appealing and spine-tingling as that might be, but to demonstrate the impact of losses. The true lesson is a stark one—losing even 10 percent in any given year can dramatically affect your portfolio and is the surest way to spending your retirement age asking folks "do you want fries with that?"

The roar of bear markets notwithstanding, stocks do provide the best investment return for investors. The historical performance record of U.S. asset returns is detailed on the next page (table 1.2). Four basic categories are considered: U.S. Treasury bill returns, long-term U.S. government bond returns, long-term corporate bond returns, and the S&P 500 stock index return. These asset classes are informally organized by risk. That is, most people would consider U.S. Treasury bill returns relatively risk-free compared to a portfolio of stocks.

Historical Returns for Different Investments
Annualized Returns through 2005 *

	Last 50 Years (annual)	Last 20 Years (annual)	Last 10 Years (annual)
S&P 500	11.3%	13.8%	10.9%
U.S. LT Corporate	6.4%	10.9%	8.2%
U.S. LT Treasury	6.6%	10.1%	8.4%
U.S. 30-Day T-Bills	5.2%	6.6%	4.7%
U.S. Inflation	4.0%	3.6%	2.7%

* Table 1.2, Source: Roger G. Ibbotson and Rex A. Sinquefield, "Stocks, Bonds, Bills, and Inflation: Year-by-Year Historical Returns," University of Chicago Press Journal of Business 2006.

One of the main exercises in finance is to understand the tradeoff between risk and return—an exercise well worth taking for average investors. Why? Because one of the assumptions that we commonly make is that investors are risk averse. That is, to get people to buy stocks as opposed to a U.S. Treasury Bond, you have to offer a higher return (to compensate them for the risk). The historical analysis of these asset classes supports the basic idea that there is a positive relation between risk and reward. That is, the higher the risk, the higher the expected return. By combining the different investments, overall risk can be reduced. This is known as asset allocation or divvying up assets among the different investment classes.

Does asset allocation help? As the table on the next page indicates (table 1.3), it does reduce chance of loss. Holding a mix of stocks and bonds provides better protection against the ravages of a bear market. But to ensure against a loss greater than 20 percent, an investor would have to maintain a 50 percent weight in both stocks and bonds. However, this strategy also has a major problem. The long-term return of a 50/50 mix of stocks and bonds drops below 9 percent. Therefore, it also is not a prudent strategy for an investor attempting to build wealth over a long time frame. This is the major fault of most financial plans written today. Most plans will include a large percentage of bonds to offset the risk of stocks. Including bonds does dilute risk, but it also dramatically reduces returns. It is not a trade-off that should be acceptable to you.

Asset Allocation History
Bear Market Test: 1926-2005 *

Stocks/Bonds	Average Return (annual)	Frequency Of Losing Years	Worst Annual Loss
100% Stock, 0% Bond	11.3%	28%	-43.1%
80% Stock, 20% Bond	10.1%	26%	-34.9%
60% Stock, 40% Bond	9.3%	24%	-26.6%
50% Stock, 50% Bond	8.8%	21%	-18.4%

* Table 1.3, Source; Roger G. Ibbotson and Rex A. Sinquefield, "Stocks, Bonds, Bills, and Inflation: Year-by-Year Historical Returns," University of Chicago Press Journal of Business 2005.

The good news is there is a solid alternative to a bond heavy portfolio. This alternative can not only prevent large losses in any given year, but also allow you to earn an annual return better than with the S&P 500 stock index. And you're about to find out how.

2

Risk & Correlation

"The only new thing in the world is the history you don't know"

—Harry S. Truman

As I discussed in Chapter 1, the stock market does not always go up. Investors who did not embrace this mantra learned their lesson in the bear market of the early 21st Century. The depth of the downturn punished those investors who ignored risk of loss. Many of the go-go stock mutual funds popularized in the late 1990s took the brunt of the fall. Although the S&P 500 stock index fell 48 percent during this period, many of the go-go mutual funds lost 75 percent or more. Imagine the dramatic impact these losses had on long-term performance calculations.

For the most part, individual investors bore heavy losses in the latest bear market because they were improperly diversified. Most of these mutual funds owned by individual investors in the late 1990s were dominated by the highest risk sector; technology. Technology stocks, as measured by the NASDAQ composite index, fell even more dramatically than the S&P 500 index. The index sank over 85 percent during the two and a half year period ending October 2002.

While the 2000-2002 period was clearly an extremely unusual investment environment, a proper investment strategy would have significantly reduced losses. The technique that accomplishes this is to carefully selecting different types of investments that have low correlations. Correlation is a measure of how frequently one event tends to happen when another event happens. High positive correlation means two events usually happen together—high SAT scores and getting through college for instance. High negative correlation means two events tend not to happen together—high SATs and a poor grade record. No correlation means the two events are independent of one another. In statistical terms two events that are perfectly correlated have a "correlation coefficient" of 1; two events that are perfectly negatively correlated have a correlation coefficient of-1; and two events that have zero correlation have a coefficient of 0.

Correlation has been used over the past twenty years by institutions and financial advisors to assemble portfolios of moderate risk. In calculating correlation, a statistician would examine the possibility of two events happening together, namely:

- If the probability of A happening is 1/X;

- And the probability of B happening is 1/Y; then

- The probability of A and B happening together is (1/X) times (1/Y), or 1/(X times Y).

There are several laws of correlation including;

1. Combining assets with a perfect positive correlation offers no reduction in portfolio risk. These two assets will simply move in tandem with each other.

2. Combining assets with zero correlation (statistically independent) reduces the risk of the portfolio. If more assets with uncorrelated returns are added to the portfolio, significant risk reduction can be achieved.

3. Combing assets with a perfect negative correlation could eliminate risk entirely. This is the principle with "hedging strategies". These strategies are discussed later in the book.

In the real world, negative correlations are very rare. Most assets maintain a positive correlation with each other. The goal of a prudent investor is to assemble a portfolio that contains uncorrelated assets. When a portfolio contains assets that possess low correlations, the upward movement of one asset class will help offset the downward movement of another. This is especially important when economic and market conditions change. As a result, including assets in your portfolio that are not highly correlated will reduce the overall volatility (as measured by standard deviation) and may also increase long-term investment returns. This is the primary argument for including dissimilar asset classes in your portfolio. Keep in mind that this type of diversification does not guarantee you will avoid a loss. It simply minimizes the chance of loss.

In table 2.1, provided by Ibbotson, the average correlation between the five major asset classes is displayed. The lowest correlation is between the U.S. Treasury Bill and the EAFE (international stocks). The highest correlation is between the S&P 500 and the EAFE; +0.77. This signifies a prominent level of correlation. Low correlations within the table appear most with U.S. Treasury Bills.

Historical Correlation of Asset Classes *

Benchmark	Return (%)	1	2	3	4	5
1 U.S. Treasury Bill	5.1	1.00				
2 U.S. LT Treasury Bond	10.1	0.23	1.00			
3 S&P 500	13.7	0.03	0.25	1.00		
4 Russell 2000	11.2	0.15	0.08	0.74	1.00	
5 MSCI EAFE	12.6	-0.13	0.22	0.77	0.57	1.00

* *Table 2.1, Source: CSAM 1985-2005*

CHANGES IN CORRELATION

Since the 1970s financial professionals have encouraged their clients to place 10-20 percent of their stock funds in international holdings. They did this to take advantage of the low historical correlation between U.S. stocks and those of their international counterparts. This is because international markets are affected by different factors than American markets and often zig while U.S. stocks zag.

Recently, however, the consensus among analysts is that globalization and other factors have caused markets to move more closely together and therefore, greatly reduced the effectiveness of diversifying overseas. A study performed by Andrew West, published in the *Capitalism Magazine*[1], examined the relationship of U.S. and international stocks for the three-year period between 12/97 to 12/00. He concluded that the correlation between the S&P 500 stock index and the international EAFE stock index was 77 percent. Recently, there have been additional published reports discounting the benefits of international diversification. These studies argue that major market correlations are rising, and therefore diversification benefits are falling. Looking at the past five years, the EAFE Index now has a correlation with the S&P 500 of 0.85. This is in contrast to earlier studies that examined correlation in the 1970s and early 1980s. These studies demonstrated that international markets had consistent low correlations; ranging from a low 0.30 percent to 0.60 percent.

This rise of correlation is due to many factors. Companies must now compete globally, not just domestically. Trade barriers have been dramatically reduced over the past ten years. This has allowed companies to cross borders with a competitively priced product. The composition of the global stock indexes like the EAFE has also changed. The EAFE is now dominated by large global companies that compete within similar industries. There are other factors as well. There is considerable

---

1.   "International Markets Handle American Political Risk" *Capitalism Magazine*, November 13, 2000

progress being made towards the alignment of regulations and corporate governance across the world. Areas under consolidation include accounting standards, treatment of minority shareholders, mergers and acquisitions, and shareholder value. As one illustration, the European Commission has proposed that all companies adopt International Accounting Standards by 2005, and Japan is moving in the same general direction. In addition, data from major exchanges indicate that foreign ownership of stocks—while still relatively modest—is rising quickly.

Foreign owners hold about 20 percent of the stocks traded on the Tokyo Stock Exchange and about 10 percent of U.S.-traded stocks. In Europe, companies are increasingly purchasing stocks across the 12 countries of in the European Union rather than in just their own. Finally, in recent years, investment managers and brokerage firms have been structuring their research activities globally, so that the same group of analysts follows a given industry across all markets. This has helped to increase the similarities in stock behavior across borders.

Many large U.S. companies count two-thirds or more of their revenues from outside the U.S. Coca-Cola, McDonald's, Texaco, and Texas Instruments are all companies that generate more than half of their revenue outside the U.S. Soon, the barriers across borders will continue to dissipate. The home country of the firm will no longer be as relevant as the global economy expands. In addition, the barriers between the stock markets will drop. I expect a global stock exchange within the next ten years. This will only encourage further correlation among international markets.

Increased correlation does not mean you should avoid international stocks. This is because the U.S. has become a much smaller part of the world economy. The simple fact is that the world is changing. Consider the following:

- The United States now accounts for only 25 percent of global output.

- The capitalization of the U.S. stock market has been reduced from 55 percent to 37 percent of world stock markets in the past fifteen years.

- The dollar has fallen against the Euro by more than 40 percent during the past two years

- More than 75 percent of all publicly traded companies are located outside the U.S.

- Growth rates in other countries can be two to three times higher than the in U.S.

FACT: In the last ten years, the U.S. has never been the world's best performing stock market

Other facts:

- During the 1980s, the Europe, and Far East Index grew 27 percent compared to 16 percent for the S&P 500 Index.

- Within the past ten years, the U.S. was among the top-four-performing markets only once (1995).

- In 2003, the S&P 500 index rebounded nicely but it was still beaten by 30 international markets. Here's a few: Sweden, up 61 percent, Germany, up 60 percent, Austria, up 54 percent, Spain, up 55 percent, India, up 75 percent.

All these statistics indicate that investing outside the United States makes sense. However, with global correlations rising, a more prudent approach should be utilized. The smartest choice for an individual in the 21st century is sector investing.

3

Sector Investing

"The study of history, while it does not endow with prophecy, may indicate lines of probability"

—*John Steinbeck*

Historically, sectors have been reasoned to be relatively less important than other factors in analyzing stock returns. Sector investing, or separating the investment universe by the major sectors of the economy (i.e. healthcare, technology, industrials, etc), has always been viewed skeptically by major university researchers. The most prominent studies demonstrating sector unimportance were published in the 1970s. In his seminal research on the gains from international diversification, Bruno Solnik (1974)[1] demonstrated that diversification across the various developed countries provides greater risk reduction than diversification across the major sectors of an economy.

Donald Lessard (1974, 1976)[2] confirmed his results, suggesting that country factors were the dominant driver in security price returns. Accepting these conclusions, traditional financial planners and investment managers have adopted country selection as a critical tactical decision for international investments. However, recent studies exam-

---

1. Bruno Solnik, "Why Not Diversify Internationally Rather Than Domestically?" *Financial Analysts Journal*, July/August 1974.
2. Lessard, Donald (1974). "World, National, and Industry Factors in Equity Returns," Journal of Finance 24: 379-91. (1976). "World, Country, and Industry Relationships in Equity Returns," Financial Analysts Journal 32: 2-8.

ining the country versus sector relationship have put these former findings in doubt.

A year 2000 study[3] performed by Brinson Partners in association
with Duke University examined a factor model for twenty-one countries that comprise the current MSCI World Developed Markets universe. The study covered 21 developed equity markets for the period
December 1985 through November 1999. Their results concluded
that sectors have become an increasingly important component of
security returns. More importantly, diversification across sectors actually provides greater risk reduction benefits than diversification across
countries. Brinson also commented that given the increasing geographical integration of markets, they expected these phenomena to persist
and even strengthen. This is due to the sea change in the economic
environment known as globalization.

Influence of Stock Performance *

	Jan-95	Jun-04
Company specific	54%	52%
Global sector influence	7%	18%
Local market influence	23%	15%
Global market influence	16%	15%

*   Table 3.1, Source: Goldman Sachs Research, August 2004

The Brinson study is not the only one that confirms the altering
landscape in sector investing. Recent research published by Goldman
Sachs reviewed the significance of sectors. Their study demonstrated
that the effect of global sector movements on individual stocks now
outweighs local market influences (see table 3.1 above). In January

---

3.   S. Cavaglia, C. Brightman, M. Aked (2000). "On the Increasing Importance
     of Industry Factors: Implications for Global Portfolio Management"

1995, global sector influences accounted for just 7 percent of individual stock performance around the world. Local market influences accounted for 23 percent, and the global market factor for 16 percent. The remaining 54 percent of stock variation could be put down to factors affecting specific companies.

But by mid-2004, the global sector effect had increased to 18 percent and was more important than either the local market (15 percent) or global market (15 percent) effects. The stock-specific influence has stayed at the same level (52 percent). This clearly demonstrates that a company's sector has become more important to its performance than the stock market of the country in which it's based. As trade barriers have fallen, economies have become more global, and company performance has become increasingly dependent on sector performance, rather than geographic location.

INVESTOR IMPLICATIONS

The new research has validated that Wall Street and foreign bourses are now three times more likely to move in lockstep. Non-geographic factors such as competitive profile, product quality and management are now critical ingredients in the investment process. The global economic and financial environment has evolved considerably since the 1970s. Today, it is uncommon to find successful large companies that do not operate on a global scale. Cross-border merger and acquisition activity is increasingly blurring the distinction between domestic and foreign companies. The long post-war trend toward a free–trade environment, including trade agreements such as GATT, NAFTA, the EC, and the World Trade Organization has dramatically raised the proportion of world GDP that is involved in international trade.

An investor examining the movements of the global stock markets in the past five years would notice a subtle change. Note the events that have taken place over the past few years. When America's tech-laden Nasdaq composite index fell dramatically in 2000, so did Europe's

Euro-tech index, Japan's Jasdaq, and Korea's Kosdaq. When U.S. firm Merck announced trouble with Vioxx in 2004, global pharmaceutical stocks such as AstraZeneca and GlaxoWelcome also fell. A portfolio that contained international stocks, therefore, was no better off than one that only contained U.S. stocks. Despite the implications of recent studies, most financial professionals still recommend international stocks as an excellent diversification tool. International stocks can provide exceptional diversification to a portfolio, but only if an investor also considers the now dominant sector influence. I offer the following conclusion;

An international mutual fund will only offer compelling diversification benefits if its largest holdings are *not* in the same sector as a U.S. based mutual fund

For example, let us look once again at hypothetical investor Joe. Joe owns a U.S. growth stock mutual fund. The mutual fund maintains a 40 percent weight in the technology sector, a 25 percent weight in the financial sector, and a 15 percent stake in the energy sector. Joe is examining 2 international mutual funds that maintain the following sector weights:

Fund A: 40% healthcare, 25% consumer, 15% financials.
Fund B: 40% technology, 25% energy, and 15% financials.

His choice should be Fund A. Fund A offers the best sector diversification for his current portfolio. Fund B maintains the same high exposure to technology stocks. It also maintains a high exposure to energy, which Joe already has in his U.S. growth stock fund. The correlation of his U.S. fund and the international fund B will no doubt be very high, probably above 0.80 percent. Choosing fund B will offer negligible diversification benefit.

Despite the growing evidence of sector importance, most financial professionals fail to diagnose such potential pitfalls for their clients. Unfortunately, they are usually unaware of the growing body of new research dispelling simplistic international exposure. Astute investors should view sector investing as the key selection criteria in the asset allocation process.

MAJOR SECTORS

There are eight major sectors of the economy; Basic Materials, Consumer Discretionary, Consumer Staple, Financial, Health Care, Industrial, Energy, and Technology. Sector & Industry Group Listing:

Sector	Industry Groups
Basic Materials:	Chemicals
	Metals & Mining
	Steel

Most of the companies here produce commodities whose sale price tends to converge with the cost of production, especially in the low-inflation environment as we have seen in recent years. These companies generally maintain high debt levels and poor long-term growth characteristics. The sector can perform well during periods of high inflation.

Consumer Discretionary:	Autos
	Building & Construction
	Publishing
	Retail

As with capital goods, these stocks perform poorly heading into economic slowdowns and perform well in expanding economies. This sector is less sensitive to overall interest rates (consumers buy homes, cars and furnishings very happily on credit while corporate purchasers worry about budgets). Many attractive investments can be found within this sector.

Consumer Staples:

Beverages
Food
Tobacco

This sector is traditionally recession-proof (consumers buy toothpaste and beer no matter what the state of the economy). The consumer group companies are not as attractive as other sectors due to their low margins, high cost of labor, and poor growth prospects. They can, however, serve as a solid defensive investment during poor economic times.

Industrial:

Aerospace/Defense
Electrical
Machinery

The industrial sector is basically the "old economy" stocks. This group is in its mature stage; with limited catalysts for future growth. Although this sector can have exceptional investment returns in economic recoveries, overall performance is expected to be sub-par.

Energy:

Oil & Gas
Drillers

The energy sector has a different dynamic than the basic materials group because of the regulation by the OPEC cartel. Large multinational companies are generally relatively unaffected by changes in the price of oil because of extensive hedging operations. The energy sector has been one of the most compelling sectors over the past three years as oil prices have climbed. Many energy stocks are also attractive for their higher than average dividend yields.

Healthcare:

Pharmaceuticals
Hospitals
Medical Devices

Companies in this sector also are relatively recession-proof—when you need medicine you need medicine. Conventional pharmaceutical companies offer relatively predictable returns. Biotech companies offer outsize returns with higher risks. Hospitals, HMOs and other care facilities offer further diversification within the sector.

Financials: Banks
Insurance Companies
Brokers

Stock prices in this sector used to be tightly correlated with changes in interest rates. In recent years, the companies have become more adept at managing interest-rate risk, but the stock prices still tend to move higher when rates move lower. Consolidation and cost control have been much bigger drivers of financial stock prices in recent years.

Banks and finance companies tend to do poorly heading into recessions, as bad loans increase and as transaction income dries up. Insurance companies, particularly property and casualty companies, suffer when underwriting competition drives down premiums.

Technology: Semiconductors
Computer
Internet
Software

Growth in this sector is subject to the same pressures as other capital goods, but demand for technology remains above the norm. Even when overall demand is high, companies are at great risk from "paradigm shifts" (e.g., mainframe computers supplanted by desktop computers). The sector is considered the most volatile of all areas of the economy.

SECTOR SELECTION

When choosing among the various sectors listed above, I focused on two specific criteria;

1. *Superior historical investment returns*

2. *Low correlations with other sectors*

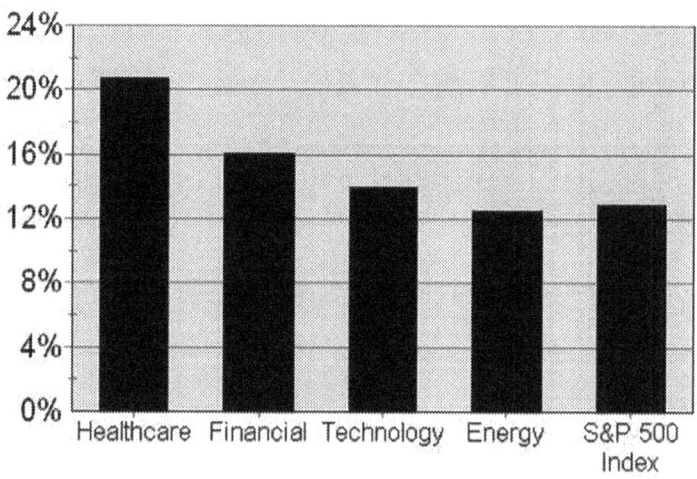

Table 3.2, Source: Lipper Inc; A Reuters Company., January 1, 1976 through December 31st, 2005. Annualized Returns. Financials measured by Financial Services Funds, Healthcare by Healthcare/ Biotechnology funds and Comstock (1976-1981), Energy by Natural Resources Funds, and Technology by Science and Technology Funds.

In table 3.2 above, three sectors (healthcare, financials, technology) outperformed the S&P 500 stock index for the 29 year period ending December 31st, 2005. All the other major sectors had annual returns below that of the S&P 500 stock index. Due to this remarkable performance, I recommend these three sectors be incorporated into a diversified portfolio. Healthcare, which maintained the largest annualized performance gain and impressive bear market protection, should be the principal sector in your portfolio.

I have also added another sector to the recommendation. My fourth recommendation, energy, is based upon the solid diversification benefits the sector maintains. Energy stocks provide an excellent choice based upon their low correlation to the other three sectors. They also provide a portfolio hedge against inflation. Inflation has an adverse impact on the stock market. In the last two periods of high inflation (1974, 1979), stocks performed very poorly. I view the energy sector as a key ingredient in a diversified portfolio.

I recommend investments within the other major sectors of the S&P 500 be limited to 10 percent of a portfolio. Although there are always excellent investment opportunities within the other major sectors, you should focus your dollars only on the superlative sectors. Based on the performance statistics, it seems logical that any investor would seriously consider only investing in my recommended 4 sectors. However, risk must also be considered. How does this strategy when evaluated on a risk-adjusted basis? Actually, it looks quite good. The reason is the low historical correlations that these four sectors possess. Here are the correlations for these four major sectors.

SECTOR	FINANCIALS	HEALTHCARE	ENERGY	TECHNOLOGY
Financials	1.00	0.64	0.45	0.30
Health Care		1.00	0.19	0.07
Energy			1.00	0.02
Technology				1.00

* *Table 3.3 Source: MSCI World, 1975-2005*

The highest correlated sectors are healthcare and financials; with a 0.64 correlation. This is considered moderately high. However, all other correlations within the chart are at a 0.45 or less. Some relationships are exceptionally low. Healthcare and technology have a minuscule 0.07 correlation. Energy and healthcare have a diminutive 0.19 correlation. These low correlations mean that although these sectors offer high performance, they do so at different times. Therefore, if healthcare stocks do exceptionally well, one or more of the other sectors are likely doing poorly. This see-saw relationship actually lowers volatility. Due to these findings, these four sectors, in combination, offer an investor a true path to high returns, with lower risk.

4

A New Investment Strategy

"Tis the part of a wise man to keep himself today for tomorrow, and not venture all his eggs in one basket."
—**Don Quizote** by Miguel de Cervantes Saavedra (1547–1616), Spanish
novelist, poet

Traditional asset allocation is outdated. As discussed in Chapter 3, new developments within the global stock markets are changing the investment landscape. Correlations within international markets are increasing. Sectoral factors are now becoming a critical element of investing. Commonly held truisms regarding traditional asset allocation are now being unmasked. Don't panic. Investors can still reap the rewards of proper diversification—but doing so takes a smarter strategy. Based on new research published over the past ten years, I believe a new investment style for the 21st century is appropriate.

1. **Concentrate your portfolio on the large, industry-leading equities within the four premier sectors of the global economy; healthcare, financials, technology, and energy. Healthcare should account for the largest weight in your portfolio due to its exceptional long-term returns and terrific defensive attributes.**

2. **To protect against the ravages of a bear stock market, the remaining balance of your portfolio should be divided among**

three income-producing investments; REIT's, U.S. 5-Year Treasury bonds, and international bonds.

3. Continue to invest internationally, but primarily within the four major sectors recommended. International stocks should weight 20-30 percent of your portfolio.

4. Avoid small cap company stocks.

There are three major reasons for these recommendations ;

1. Certain sectors within the economy outperform others over time.

2. Sectors are becoming more relevant in diversifying a portfolio.

3. Small company shares do not outperform larger company shares and have substantial periods of underperformance (see Chapter 12).

SECTOR CONCENTRATION

I recommend you allocate the majority of your stock dollars to four sectors of the economy; healthcare, financials, technology, and energy. The healthcare sector should account for 40 percent of your portfolio. An additional 40 percent of your account should be devoted to the other three major sectors; financials, technology, and energy.

This unique sectoral approach is recommended for three reasons;

1. Each sector has demonstrated superior performance over the past thirty years.

2. Each sector has exceptional long-term future potential due to changing demographics and increased globalization of the major economies.

3. **Each sector provides substantial diversification benefits for a portfolio.**

I recommend a small portion of your stock holdings (up to 10 percent) be selected from other sectors of the S&P 500; i.e. consumer staples, and certain retail, media, and consumer discretionary firms.

Strong consumer companies such as Proctor & Gamble and Wrigley can offer one of the most compelling investment options outside my four recommended sectors. Many of these firms can grow earnings 10 percent or more. They also maintain reasonable valuation metrics. The most important attribute is the safety they provide for a diversified portfolio. You should select these firms based upon the safety rating of the company. These companies should maintain a rating of 1 for safety by Value Line (www.valueline.com). These selections will serve as a bedrock for your portfolio, further protecting your account from a significant loss during a bear stock market.

In choosing stock investments for your portfolio, I recommend:

1. **Maintain a 35 stock portfolio.**

2. **Each stock purchase should have an initial weight of 2.5 percent.**

3. **If a stock reaches a 5 percent weight, reduce your position to minimize risk.**

4. **If a stock falls by 25 percent, re-evaluate. If something fundamentally within the company has changed, sell. If the decline in stock price is due to the entire sector being out of favor, buy more and average up.**

These rules provide an additional risk reduction. Stock concentration is equally as damaging as sector concentration. These rules strive to take the psychological effects out of the decision making process. These set of laws prevents an investor from "falling in love" with any one stock. In general, most investors tend to believe they are infallible. Even seasoned professionals make investment mistakes every day.

A 35 STOCK PORTFOLIO

Considering that most stock mutual funds contain over 100 stocks, a 35 stock portfolio might seem very risky. However, research has once again refuted common wisdom. Ben Graham, one of the founders of modern securities analysis, counseled in his classic 1949 treatise on stock investing for individuals, *The Intelligent Investor*, that adequate, but not excessive, diversification ranges between 10 and 30 stocks.

Graham's instincts were more or less confirmed 20 years later, when "Diversification and the Reduction of Dispersion: An Empirical Analysis," an early academic inquiry into diversification by J. Evans and S.H. Archer, appeared in the Journal of Finance in December 1968. The paper found that with as little as 10 randomly selected stocks, and no more than 15, the benefit of diversification (measured by the reduction of standard deviation) is virtually exhausted.

Standard Deviations of Annual Portfolio Returns [*]

# of Stocks	Average SD of annual portfolio returns	Ratio of Portfolio SD to SD of a single stock
1	49.24%	1.00
10	23.93%	0.49
30	20.87%	0.42
50	20.20%	0.41
100	19.69%	0.40
300	19.34%	0.39
500	19.27%	0.39
1,000	19.21%	0.39

* Table 4.1—Meir Statman, "How Many Stocks Make a Diversified Portfolio?" Journal of Financial and Quantitative Analysis 22 (September 1987), pp. 353–64. They were derived from E. J. Elton and M. J. Gruber, "Risk Reduction and Portfolio Size: An Analytic Solution," Journal of Business 50 (October 1977), pp. 415–37.

Another study published 20 years later by Meir Statman confirmed these findings as well. This data is presented in table 4.1 This academic study examined what is known as random diversification. Random diversification is the act of diversifying without regard to relevant investment characteristics such as investment return or sector classification. What Statman found is that even randomly diversified portfolios start to reduce risk dramatically at about 10 stocks. Risk in his study was measured by standard deviation—a measure of how annual investment returns were dispersed.

Note the dramatic drop in standard deviation as each stock is added. Risk substantially declines as an investor migrates from 1 stock to 10. However, the marginal risk reduction benefits become smaller and smaller as more stocks are added. Therefore, no matter how many stocks are tacked on, the overall risk will not decline by any significant amount. Mr. Statman came to the conclusion that 30 to 40 stocks offered the best risk/reward scenario.

Not everyone has accepted the idea that diversification takes as little as 35 stocks. Several studies over the years have found that the 20-to-30-securities rule of thumb is flawed. A recent study done by John Campbell at Harvard University demonstrated that such small portfolios are questionable. This is due to the fact that stock volatility has increased. His study conclusion; it takes a portfolio of 50 stocks to reduce excess risk to 5 percent. However, although his study found that 93 percent of the diversification benefits are achieved with a portfolio of 50 stocks; the figure drops to only 90 percent at the 35 stock range.

The reason for this slight difference between a 30 and 50 stock portfolio is that although volatility increased, correlation actually decreased over time. A typical U.S. stock had a correlation between 0.25 and 0.30 with other stocks in the 1960s, but by the late 1990's this correlation had fallen below 0.10. So despite the evidence of more volatility of individual stocks, stocks now have lower correlations. Therefore, I believe a portfolio of 35 stocks, diversified between the sectors of healthcare, financials, technology, and energy, provides more than enough diversification.

5

Healthcare Sector

"Be careful about reading health books, You may die of a misprint"
—Mark Twain

The U.S. healthcare industry is the largest single slice of the U.S. economy, amounting to expenditures of $1.5 trillion in 2005. The health care sector is quite diverse and includes pharmaceutical companies, healthcare facilities, managed care/HMOs, medical supply manufacturers, and biotechnology. Each of these sub-sectors is affected by different issues, but all share a common goal—to profit while preserving or restoring the health of their clients.

This sector represents 12.4 percent of the market capitalization of the S&P 500, making it the fourth largest sector. The healthcare sector has delivered exceptional investment returns over the 29 year period ending December 31st, 2005. As demonstrated in Chapter 4, the category's returns, as measured by the Lipper Healthcare Funds average and Comstock, have been the highest of any sector; a 20.7 percent annual return. Just as important are the defensive characteristics. Since 1976, the healthcare sector has only suffered five losing years (see table 5.1 below). This is the lowest number of negative return years of any of the major sectors within the S&P 500 stock index. The sector also faired well in 1990, 1994, and 2000—losing years in the general market. Healthcare stocks generally outperform the market when the economy is sluggish and many other stocks are losing value.

Healthcare Sector: Losing Years since 1976

1984	-2.19%
1987	-1.16%
1992	-6.65%
2001	-12.55%
2002	-18.85%

Table 5.1, Source: Lipper Inc; A Reuters Company., January 1, 1976 through December 31st, 2005. Healthcare returns measured by the Lipper Index of Healthcare/Biotechnology Funds and Comstock (1976-1981)

DEMOGRAPHICS

One of the major supports of the healthcare sector is the graying of America—and the world. It renders healthcare a true long-term growth story. The world's population is simply getting older, and this will lead to increased demand for, and greater spending on, healthcare solutions. Growth will also be boosted as standards and expectations rise, generating demand for better equipment, technologies and procedures. Healthcare economics will be dramatically shaped by the march of the baby boom generation toward retirement age. According to data from the U.S. Administration on Aging, people aged 65 years and older consume 4 times as much healthcare per capita as people under 65. When Medicaid and Medicare programs were enacted in the 1960s, the 65+ age group constituted 10 percent of the total population. This number has grown to 12.8 percent of the total in 2006. Despite this relatively modest increase, healthcare expenditures soared during this time frame due to technological increases that led to new drugs and procedures.

In coming years, we face an acceleration of growth in the ranks of the elderly. By 2010, the population of the 65+ group is estimated to grow to 40.1 million from 35.3 million in 2000. Between 2010 and 2020, these numbers will swell to 53.3 million. Therefore, the 65+ group will grow to 16.3 percent of the total U.S. population in 2020.

The Labor Department's outlook projects that the labor force will continue to age along with the Baby Boomers through 2014. The number of workers in the 55 and older group is expected to increase 4.1% annually, more than four times faster than the overall labor force, which should increase 1% per year, the same as the growth in the working age population, and a considerable slowing from previous decades. The labor force participation rate of workers older than 55 has been increasing since the mid-1980s and is projected to continue increasing at least to 2014. Older workers are living longer, so they have to work longer to support themselves and to have health care benefits. The demand for health care—which currently accounts for a record 21 percent of consumer spending on goods and services—will continue to boom throughout the next several decades. Simply, as our country ages, individuals will need more medical care, providing consistent demand for new health care products and services.

REGULATORY FACTORS

Outside of the U.S., most healthcare expenditures have come under nearly complete government control. The U.S. has the lone remaining predominantly private healthcare system among developed countries. However, the largest single payer in our system is the Federal Government; through its Medicare and Medicaid programs. As a result, healthcare economics are increasingly governed by public policy, which is influenced by societal opinion, budgetary constraint, and tax policy. Demographic, social and political trends are likely to increase government's role as a payer of health care costs. As costs increase and the population ages, the government will take on a larger role in the healthcare sector. Changes in government reimbursement, taxation, research rules, or FDA drug application processing make it more or less economically appealing to invest in new healthcare products, drugs, new drug research, etc. Future problems ranging from presidential efforts to revamp the entire health system, to federal and state laws that alter reimbursement rules, to slow approval of new drugs by the Food and Drug Administration could all have a dramatic impact on the healthcare sector.

ECONOMIC FACTORS

Healthcare sector stocks are generally non-cyclical (or at any rate, less cyclical) because the demand for healthcare products and drugs doesn't depend on the state of the economy. Over the past ten years, the healthcare sector has enjoyed stable investment returns despite the economic environment. Economic forecasts for moderate growth and declining interest rates are advantageous for the health care industry in general. When growth is moderate and money is tight, consumers may put off buying new cars and computers, but they will nevertheless continue to pay for medicines and health services. The sector tends to do best when the economy is sluggish or in recession.

SUB-SECTOR ANALYSIS

The pharmaceutical industry comprises 5 percent of the benchmark S&P 500 index and accounts for the majority of the stock market capitalization in the healthcare sector. Pharmaceutical companies sell products necessary for health—not for some discretionary need. These products usually represent a must-repeat purchase, no matter the economic situation. Pharmaceutical companies are among the best-known firms operating within the healthcare sector. They include giants like Pfizer and Merck, which make drugs such as Lipitor and Zocor. One of the major challenges facing pharmaceutical firms is increased competition from generic drug manufacturers. The Food and Drug Administration (FDA) has estimated that over the next five years, 858 drugs will lose patent protection, opening the doors to generic competition. Other issues that surfaced in 2004 are safety related. With the recent problems with Cox-2 drugs such as Vioxx, the FDA is under increased scrutiny to ensure the safety of new drugs. Drug companies have historically maintained high margins. Gross margins average 70 percent and operating margins usually range above 30 percent, which is twice that of the average S&P 500 company.

Pharmaceutical companies' high margins are dependent on exclusive rights to market the products of their costly research efforts. Patent protection usually guarantees high margins on new drugs for at least a decade. When patents expire, generic drug manufacturers erode pharmaceutical companies' profits by selling comparable drugs at discounts of 80 to 90 percent. Most of the major drug makers are based in the U.S. due to our favorable patent laws. In addition, the U.S. is the only major drug market in the world without government price controls.

The healthcare facilities industry includes hospitals, acute care, rehabilitation, nursing homes, assisted living facilities, and home healthcare services. Major players in this sub-sector include Tenet, HCA, Health Management Associates, and Manor Care. Healthcare service providers have suffered almost two decades of increasingly restrictive reimbursement policies from both government and private insurers. Reimbursement for services has been particularly brutal in the past 5 years. Physicians have endured significant cuts in income, nursing home and home healthcare providers have been put in financial intensive care, and hospitals were plunged into increasing distress. Recently, the government has added back funding to this distressed industry, improving the fundamentals of the major players.

The managed care/HMO industry is distinguished from a traditional fee-for-service (or indemnity) health insurer in that a managed care company attempts to actively manage the cost and quality of healthcare. The major players in this industry include Aetna, Cigna, and Wellpoint. The managed care industry is composed of a continuum of plans exercising various degrees of cost and control. Listed from least to most controlled are managed indemnity plans, preferred provider orga-

nizations (PPO), point-of-service (POS) plans, and health mainte-
nance organizations (HMO). HMOs are fighting their own battles
with Congress; Medicare reform and a Patient's Bill of Rights. The
Patient's Bill of Rights would be detrimental to HMOs because it
could give consumers greater power to sue.

The medical products and supplies industry includes manufacturers and
distributors of products and supplies used in health care delivery,
including surgical and medical instruments; orthopedic devices and
surgical supplies; diagnostic reagents; electro-medical equipment; x-ray
equipment; and dental equipment. Depending on the degree of technology elements in these products, they can be further grouped into
two distinct sub-sectors: conventional hospital supplies, and medical
technology products.

Conventional hospital supplies account for 40 percent of the industry's total worldwide sales. This market is dominated by a relatively
small number of large manufacturers including Cardinal Health,
McKesson, and AmerisourceBergen. Medical technology products
control a relatively small share of the market and serve a specialized
patient population, but have much higher profit margins. The two-tier
industry is dominated by a few leading manufacturers such as Boston
Scientific, Baxter International, Medtronic, and Becton Dickinson,
who offer a comprehensive line of both conventional hospital supplies
and technology products to a broad market segment. A larger number
of companies in this industry are small and medium-sized firms that
produce limited lines of specialty medical devices and products.

The biotechnology industry has a history of less than 3 decades. It is different from traditional pharmaceutical industry primarily in the technology employed. Biotechnology involves using recombinant DNA
technology to manipulate living organisms or biological components at
cellular, subcellular, or molecular levels to create marketable products
for human or animal health needs. The rapid advance in biomedical

and molecular cellular biology research has ushered in a new wave of biotechnology. The combination of genome research and information technology has created an exciting new technology frontier, bioinformatics, which promises a revolution in the way diseases will be treated. As more and more traditional pharmaceutical companies are engaged in biological drug discovery, the line between the pharmaceutical and biotechnology firms is becoming less clear. Currently, Amgen is the only biotech company listed in the S&P 500 Index. Other large firms in this arena include Biogen IDEC and Genentech.

INVESTING IN THE HEALTHCARE SECTOR

The healthcare sector should represent 40 percent of your overall stock portfolio. This large weight reflects the fact that the sector provides an exceptional long-term investment return with terrific defensive characteristics. This sector will perform best during a recession and offset losses in the more economically sensitive sectors; financials and technology. Stock selection within the healthcare sector should concentrate on pharmaceuticals, with the balance of money in the four other sub-sectors listed above.

Table 5.2 provides you with the major companies within the healthcare sector. Ten to twelve stocks should be chosen from this list. In choosing an individual stock from the healthcare list, consider the following;

- *Concentration should be in pharmaceuticals*

- *Select companies of a large size (5 billion market cap >).*

- *Favor industry leaders within each sub-sector.*

- *Attempt to add to your portfolio sub-sectors that are out of favor (see Chapter 11)*

• *Add to healthcare when the economy is near the end of an economic boom. If the Federal Reserve starts raising interest rates, increase exposure to healthcare.*

Healthcare Stocks	Market Cap
Abbott Labs	60,508
Allergan	7,597
AmerisourceBergen	7,729
Amersham PLC ADR	5,223
Amgen	65,231
AstraZeneca PLC ADR	57,260
Baxter International	18,252
Becton Dickinson	7,830
Biogen IDEC	11,500
Biomet	7,399
Boston Scientific	17,969
Bristol-Myers Squibb	49,007
Cardinal Health	26,462
Chiron	7,312
Cigna	6,296
Eisai ADR	9,871
Eli Lilly & Company	73,480
Forest Laboratories	22,603
Genentech	50,068
Genzyme Corporation General	7,525
Gilead Sciences	16,057
GlaxoSmithKline ADR	58,273

Health Management	5,889
HCA	22,116
IDEC Pharmaceuticals	6,309
Johnson & Johnson	160,283
Luxottica Group ADR	6,011
McKesson	8,346
MedImmune	7,555
Medtronic	56,126
Merck	127,368
Novartis ADR	107,099
Novo Nordisk ADR	15,043
Pfizer	187,946
Pharmacia	53,759
Quest Diagnostics	5,744
Roche Holding ADR	64,002
Sanofi-Aventis ADR	39,680
Schering-Plough	31,320
Smith & Nephew ADR	13,499
St. Jude Medical	7,165
Stryker	13,136
Takeda Chemical ADR	24,566
Tenet Healthcare	5,082
Teva Pharmaceutical	9,840
UnitedHealth Group	48,132
WellPoint Health	10,122

Wyeth	48,068
Zimmer Holdings	11,582

* Table 5.2. Source: Value Line
Market Cap is presented in millions

6
The Financial Sector

"I'd like to live like a poor man with lots of money"

—Pablo Picasso

The financial services industry is an important facilitator of economic activity. The primary function of any financial institution is to expedite the exchange of financial resources between savers and borrowers. The financial services sector includes 5 sub-sectors; banks, insurance companies, consumer financial services, securities companies, and S&Ls. Overall, the financial sector includes over 6,400 stocks. The sector represents 21.1 percent of the market capitalization of the S&P 500, making it the largest sector of the index.

The category's returns, as measured by the Lipper Financial Services Funds Average, have been impressive for the 29-year period ending December 31st, 2005, a 16 percent annualized return. Remarkably, a substantial proportion of the category's long-term gains has come not from small, high-risk companies, but from established, highly visible, and financially sound firms like Citigroup, Fannie Mae, and Merrill Lynch. Looking forward, there are three compelling reasons for sustained outperformance of the financial services sector; demographics, globalization, and low interest rates.

DEMOGRAPHICS

Data from the U.S. Census Bureau indicate that the number of Americans in the 45 to 64 group is estimated to increase nearly 47% from 2000 to 2015. It is expected that during the next ten years, a U.S. citizen has turned 50 once every eight seconds. Concerned about the reliability of Social Security, this group is just now taking control of their financial future. The vast majority are approaching their 50s and will have an increasing need for financial and retirement services from tax planning to investment management services. Baby boomers have historically undersaved for retirement. Financial firms should benefit heavily from this trend over the ensuing 15 years.

GLOBALIZATION

The continued development of foreign economies will spur demand for investment, insurance, and banking services. Global financial institutions that anticipate the impending boom will be the best prepared for this tremendous opportunity over the next ten years. With regulatory constraints relaxed, banks and other financial service companies will be able to offer an even wider array of financial products to an ever-growing client base.

Due to the high costs of state pensions, governments outside the United States have no choice but to liberalize their pension systems and privatize pension management. This will create an enormous demand for wealth-building investments, retirement funding options, insurance, and personal financial advisory services. The marketplaces in Europe, Japan, and in key economies elsewhere will be prime targets of business expansion. Alliances and partnerships between trusted brands will be extremely powerful. In addition, mergers will continue to accelerate as financial firms looking to gain exposure to these markets make unsolicited bids. In the years to come, the global financial markets will most likely be dominated by a relatively few large multinational financial companies capable of attaining enormous economies of scale, while offering a broad portfolio of products to service the growing demands of their client base.

LOW INTEREST RATES

The financial services sector's high investment return has been aided in no small part by a long-term decline in interest rates from their highs in 1981. Lower rates have generally meant lower funding costs for banking and investment institutions. They have also encouraged investors to search the stock and bond markets for alternatives to lower-yielding traditional savings accounts. Although the decline in rates is most likely over, interest rates are expected to remain stable over the next several years. If interest rates do climb, financial firms such as regional banks and thrifts will suffer the most as interest spreads between long-term and short-term rates decline.

ECONOMIC FACTORS

As a whole, the financial sector is highly sensitive to the health of the economy. Interest rates in particular tend to play a leading role in determining the short-term price movements of financial stocks. Interest rates impact financial firms through a variety of methods. Rising interest rates in general slow down economic growth, reducing demand for financial services such as loans. Higher rates can also lead to higher loan defaults, and corresponding damage to a lender's bottom line.

In addition, rising interest rates tend to hurt stock prices, which can also result in reduced business for firms such as investment banks. Interest income is a large portion of revenue for many financial companies, thus rate changes can flow directly to the bottom line. Other economic indicators also play a role in investors' valuations of financial companies. Factors such as GDP growth, housing starts, consumer and business confidence, purchasing indices and consumer spending can impact financial stocks on a daily basis. In many cases, these factors play a dual role: their individual impact on the selected industry or company and the anticipated impact they will have on FOMC interest rate policy.

SUB-SECTOR ANALYSIS

The banking industry (including money-center, major and regional banks) currently comprises nearly 41 percent of the S&P financial services index. The banking industry has historically been one of the most heavily regulated industries in the United States. This was a direct result of the 1929 stock market crash which resulted in hundreds of bank failures. In recent years, regulators have explored the idea of banks becoming more competitive with other types of financial service firms.

With the ratification of the Gramm-Leach-Bliley Act in 1999, the U.S. joined countries in Europe and Asia in allowing banks to expand beyond their traditional roles of collecting deposits and writing loans. This has led to the creation of financial behemoths like Citigroup, the second-largest bank by assets in the world. Other major players in this industry include JP Morgan Chase, Bank of America, Wells Fargo, and Wachovia. To boost their income outside the traditional loan segment, banks have de-emphasized lower-margin traditional banking operations to focus on more lucrative products including mutual funds and insurance products. In addition, many banks are now concentrating on technology-based activities such as transaction processing and account custody services. Most major banks, therefore, are now considered comprehensive financial institutions.

The financial services companies represent over 12 percent of the S&P 500 financial sector. It is important to point out that several of the strongest competitors in the financing business are units of larger companies in other industries, such as GE Capital Services, Ford Motor

Credit, Capital One, and GMAC, and are not technically part of the financial sector. The industry has traditionally offered automobile loans and credit cards. However, in recent years, many financial companies have offered boat and motor home loans. These upstream markets offer higher profitability to financial service companies because borrowers usually have to finance these assets for a longer period of time. An emerging trend in this sub-sector over the past few years has been to securitize the receivables of lenders. A lender pools various financial receivables and structures them as asset-backed securities and sells them to the public securities market. In turn, this process helps the finance companies manage risk exposure to single borrower, industry, product type, or concentration. Financial service company stocks tend to behave very much like banks. Because they are less safe and less regulated than banks, finance companies have greater investment risk.

The insurance industry (including Accident & Health, Life, Property-Casualty, and Multi-Line Insurance, Insurance Brokers, and Specialty Insurers) composes roughly 22 percent of the benchmark. The insurance industry (about 60 percent of worldwide premiums) has had the most profound changes in the products it sells. Over the last quarter of a century, insurers such as AIG and AXA have seen their business shift from basic insurance coverage to annuity products. This has fundamentally changed the way life insurance firms do business, as they now concentrate on managing investment risk, rather than the mortality risk of an individual.

As a result, life and accident insurance firms now compete more directly with financial services firms. Some insurance companies have even shifted their product mix to offer consumer finance and credit cards. Homeowner and auto insurance is the most important area of the property and casualty insurance business. Competition is often based on price. Property & Casualty insurers have tended to stay within their niche. The greatest potential threat may be the entry of banks into the P&C insurance business. Overall, the insurance industry is less effected by interest rates than banks and thrifts. These companies generally offer defensive characteristics during economic slowdowns. Therefore, investor exposure in this area offers an excellent diversification benefit.

The securities industry accounts for roughly 8 percent of the benchmark. Major securities firms include Merrill Lynch, Morgan Stanley, and Goldman Sachs. The securities industry is extremely vulnerable to wide swings in economic activity. During recessions, securities firms often lay off personnel because of a reduction in financial activity with new Initial Public Offerings (IPOs) and reductions in the value of stock trading activity. However, during boom times the industry is marked by substantial volumes in stock trading activity which increases demand for additional personnel to meet the rise in business.

Securities firms contribute to capital raising by assisting corporations and others in their efforts to issue debt and equity securities, and by selling these newly-created securities to individuals and institutions. Activity in these primary markets is strongly influenced by changes in interest rates. The major old-line firms have been under fire from the gradual shift from full-service to discount brokerage houses. Discount brokers execute orders at low prices and have increased their market share to 14.4 percent of retail commission revenue. Discounters consist of Charles Schwab, Ameritrade Securities, and E*Trade Group. These new securities firms have yet to enter the highly profitable IPO market, a potential risk to the established old-line players. Securities firms are the most volatile section of the financial industry. These stocks generally move up and down with the stock market, but to a much greater degree. Investors should be careful as to the timing of investing in this sector.

The S&L or thift industry represent less than 5 percent of the financial company universe and are represented by only two stocks, Washington Mutual and Golden West Financial. Thrifts primarily derive their revenue from home mortgages. Thrifts are more sensitive than banks in their sensitivity to economic factors such as interest rates. Rising interest rates can negatively affect the stock prices of thrifts.

INVESTING IN THE FINANCIAL SECTOR

The financial sector should be a 15 percent segment in your stock portfolio. The sector provides an excellent balance of risk and return. Selection within financials should cover the broad range of sub-sectors listed above. The list below provides you with the major companies within the financial sector. Nine to eleven stocks should be chosen from this list. In choosing an individual stock from the financials' list, consider the following;

- *Broadly diversify among the various sub-sectors. Any concentration should be on banks.*

- *Select companies of a large size (5 billion market cap >).*

- *Favor industry leaders within each sub-sector.*

- *Attempt to add to your portfolio sub-sectors that are out of favor (see Chapter 11).*

- *When the Federal Reserve starts raising interest rates, reduce exposure to financials. Especially avoid thrifts and brokers. Concentrate your investments on more defensive financials; insurers and regional banks.*

Financial Stocks	Market Cap
ABN Amro Bank ADR	23,706
ACE	7,467
Aegon NV ADR	18,347
Aetna	6,526
AFLAC	20,371
Allianz AG ADR	21,896
Allied Irish Banks ADR	12,463
Allstate	25,906
American Express	47,634
American International Grp	160,168
AmSouth Bancorporation	7,413
Anthem	8,517
Aon	5,459
Australia & New Zealand Bk	15,664
AXA ADR	21,942
Banco Bilbao Vizcaya ADR	31,545
Banco Santander SA ADR	31,694
Bank of America	106,248
Bank of Ireland ADR	11,013
Bank of Montreal	13,759
Bank of New York	19,102
Bank One	44,118
Barclays PLC ADR	37,470

BB&T	16,546
Bear Stearns	5,991
Berkshire Hathaway B	104,023
Canadian Imperial Bank of C	12,162
Capital One Financial	7,095
Charles Schwab	14,081
Charter One Financial	6,687
Cheung Kong Holdings ADR	15,345
Chubb	9,463
Cincinnati Financial	5,955
Citigroup	182,752
CNA Financial	5,668
Comerica	7,465
Countrywide Financial	6,711
Credit Suisse Group ADR	28,205
Deutsche Bank AG	26,803
Fannie Mae	77,811
Fifth Third Bancorp	33,034
FleetBoston Financial	28,602
Franklin Resources	8,977
Freddie Mac	44,296
Golden State Bancorp	5,042
Golden West Financial	11,506
Goldman Sachs Group	33,996
Hartford Financial Services	11,526
HSBC Holdings PLC ADR	102,006

ING Group NV ADR	32,474
J.P. Morgan Chase & Co.	50,735
Jefferson-Pilot	5,664
John Hancock Financial	8,309
KeyCorp	10,494
Lehman Brothers Holdings	13,302
Lincoln National	5,965
Manulife Financial	11,062
Marsh & McLennan Companies	24,581
Mellon Financial	11,230
Merrill Lynch & Company	34,647
Metropolitan Life Insurance	19,818
Millea Holdings ADR	11,000
Mitsubishi Tokyo ADR	28,019
Morgan Stanley	44,593
National Australia Bank ADR	27,881
National City	16,907
Nomura Holdings ADR	24,914
North Fork Bancorporation	5,412
Northern Trust	7,706
Orix ADR	5,075
PNC Financial Services	12,664
Principal Financial Group	10,039
Progressive	10,332
Prudential Financial	19,202
Prudential PLC ADR	12,152

SLM	16,722
St. Paul	7,655
State Street	13,071
SunTrust Banks	16,570
Synovus Financial	5,716
Toronto-Dominion Bank	13,145
Travelers Property Casualty	16,059
UBS AG	62,484
Union Planters	5,710
UnionBanCal	6,296
US Bancorp	42,315
Wachovia	51,556
Washington Mutual	33,667
Wells Fargo	80,032
Westpac Banking ADR	15,005
XL Capital	10,726

* Table 6.1. Source: Value Line
Market Cap is presented in millions

7

Technology Sector

"It has become appallingly obvious that our technology has exceeded our humanity"

—Albert Einstein

The technology sector is composed of 6 major industry groups, including telecommunication equipment, semiconductor and chip companies, computer hardware & storage, computer software, computer services, and internet companies. This sector is the most volatile in the stock market. The players are sensitive to technological innovations and frequently are subject to competitive changes. Advances in computer processing, network bandwidths, and internet functioning are the key drivers behind the "information age." Technology stocks represent 13.6 percent of the benchmark S&P 500 Index. This has dropped substantially since the beginning of the decade. As of January 1, 2000, the technology weight in the S&P 500 had grown to above 30 percent. The NASDAQ exchange, mainly comprised of technology companies, dropped 80 percent in value from March of 2000 to October of 2002.

With the substantial drop of the NASDAQ since 2000, technology valuations are now more appropriate and in line with historical averages. Historically, the technology sector has delivered nearly a 14 percent average return over the past 29-year period ending December 31st, 2005. I expect that the technology sector will continue to deliver excellent performance over the next decade. Advances in this sector will depend on the continued advancement of the internet and broadband services, global competition, and cellular technology.

BROADBAND & INTERNET ADVANCES

While the 1970s and 1980s will be remembered as the "Information Age," the 1990s will undoubtedly be singled out in history as the beginning of the "Internet Age." Looking forward, the 2000s may become the "Broadband Age" or even better: the "Convergence Age." The advent of the networked computer was truly revolutionary in terms of information processing, data sharing, and data storage. In the 1990s, the Internet was even more revolutionary in terms of communications at virtually all levels and in furthering the progress of data sharing, from the personal level to the global enterprise level.

Today, broadband sources such as fiber optic, satellite, and cable modem provide very high-speed access to information and media of all types via the Internet, creating an always-on environment. The result is a widespread convergence of entertainment, telephony, and computerized information: data, voice and video delivered to a rapidly-evolving array of Internet appliances, PDAs, wireless devices (including cellular telephones) and desktop computers. Such a high-speed optical connection is the equivalent of dozens of streaming video files running at once. Starting with today's very rapid implementation of cable modem access to U.S. homes, increasingly faster broadband will soon begin to change the nature of the U.S. home as well as the office.

GLOBAL COMPETITION

For businesses, the stark realities of global competition are fueling investments in technology products. Demands from customers for better service, higher quality, and depth of inventory are mercilessly driving companies to achieve efficient re-stocking, higher productivity and faster, more thorough management information. These demands will continue to intensify.

Future needs include computer networks that speed information around the globe; instant e-mail and improved long-distance telecommunications; software with the power to call up instant answers to complex questions; satellites to provide complete mobile communication; and clear, fiber optic cables that carry tens of thousands of streams of data across minuscule beams of light. Businesses are paving the paths to their futures with dollars invested in technology because: 1) resulting productivity gains create a tremendous return on investment; 2) the relative cost of the technology itself has plummeted while its power has multiplied; 3) competitive pressures leave them no choice.

ECONOMIC FACTORS

As a whole, the technology sector is highly sensitive to the health of the economy. Other economic indicators also play a role in investors' valuations of financial companies. Factors such as GDP growth, housing starts, consumer and business confidence, purchasing indices, and consumer spending can impact financial stocks on a daily basis. In many cases, these factors play a dual role: their individual impact on the selected industry or company and the anticipated impact they will have on FOMC interest rate policy.

SUB-SECTOR ANALYSIS

The telecommunications equipment industry comprises 5 percent of the benchmark S&P 500. It is a $340 billion industry providing telephony networking services to telecom service providers and business enterprises worldwide. The industry is expected to grow at a rate of 10-12 percent through 2010, with the data communications and wireless segments showing the strongest growth potential. Historically, telecom equipment giants Lucent, Nortel and Motorola have enjoyed strength in the carrier market, while computer communication equipment providers such as Cisco have staked their claim servicing the enterprise markets. The growing competition between the Telecommunication and Computer Communication equipment makers is fierce.

The idea of converging voice and data has forced companies in these two industries to re-evaluate who their competitors are. In the search for increased revenue, companies are now providing comprehensive technology equipment and services in the enterprise and carrier markets.

The semiconductor industry designs, manufactures, and sells computer components such as microprocessors, chipsets, microcontrollers, flash memory products, graphics products, network and communications products, systems management software, conferencing products and digital imaging products. The growth in the telecommunication services industry has spurred a corresponding boom in the semiconductor business. Increasing bandwidth, rather than processing power constraints are hindering PC functionality. With the greater need for bandwidth, build-out of networking infrastructure, the proliferation of the internet, and the growth of wireless communication, the semiconductor industry will face strong demand. In this space, there are a variety of major players. Intel leads sales of microprocessors and flash memories, which enable cell phones to retain numbers for redial and VCRs to remember to record ER. Advanced Micro Devices (AMD) ranks #2; Intel vs. AMD is one of the legendary rivalries of chipdom. Other key chip makers include Texas Instruments, Maxim Integrated, Analog Devices, ST Microelectronics, and Xilinx.

The semiconductor equipment industry produced $8.5 billion in sales in the first half of 2005. Applied Materials is the largest producer of the complex machinery required to make semiconductors, while Taiwan Semiconductor Manufacturing (TSMC) is the world's largest semiconductor foundry. The demand for microprocessors is fueled by the capacity and speed requirements of various computer applications.

The computer hardware & storage industry designs, manufacturers, and develops markets, services, and supports a wide range of computer systems, notebooks, and network servers that perform electronic data processing. Over the past several years, investors have favored relatively few large cap names. The largest players are Dell, EMC, IBM, Hitachi, and Hewlett Packard. In the hardware space, the continued decline in average selling prices (ASPs) in the PC market has been a significant challenge for companies in the industry for the past three years.

In the personal computer industry, software drives hardware. Unfortunately, the market has not seen a significant application since Window 95. Although the Internet remains the dominant force behind PC sales, the rise of wireless technologies and the subsequent convergence of devices like cell phones and personal digital assistants (PDAs) with personal computers may provide a new spark for the languid PC sector. The storage sector market led by EMC is comprised of companies that manufacture and/or distribute products considered as add-ons or basic components to computers, such as storage devices. Today's computers need a lot of data storage capacity in order to use more sophisticated software and operate in more complex multi-user environments. In fact, the amount of storage capacity being shipped is expected to surge exponentially over the next several years, driven in large part by e-mail and the Internet. Almost every technology trend is leading to increased demand for storage.

The computer software industry is characterized by significant expenses for up-front development, marketing, and technical support for initial versions of software products. Software companies are divided into major categories including spreadsheets, word processing, data base, utilities, graphics, and internet security. Major players include Microsoft, SAP, Oracle, and Symantec. Gross margins in the software business are often 70 to 80 percent because there is very little expense needed to support a software company.

Labor is the largest expense item since software development often involves working in teams of 6, 12, or even 100 persons. Furthermore, software projects often involve long lead times between different versions. Software publishers write application software for a specific operating system. This creates a standardized format and ensures programs work with one another. The newest trend in the software industry is to sell software as a subscription instead of in a shrink-wrapped package. This ensures continuity of revenue and lessens the wild swings in earnings that typically impact software firms.

The computer services industry has become increasingly complex in recent years thanks largely to advances in computer hardware and software technology. Major players in this sub-sector include IBM and Hewlett Packard. The major players are also manufacturers of hardware as well. In the computer services industry, outsourcing has become prevalent. It involves a customer hiring an outside computer service firm to perform either a portion of or all data processing and management needs. This allows the customer to focus on its core competencies. The vendor establishes control of a client's data processing facilities to fulfill the contract requirements.

The internet industry is characterized by rapid development of content over computer networks. The rapid pace of the internet has resulted in intense competition for web audience attention and users of internet software. The internet industry encompasses all companies engaged in creating, developing, or processing electronic information through a computer network system. Many of these companies are a direct outgrowth of the computer software industry. Major players include Google, Yahoo, and E-Bay. Most internet companies have high stock valuations and very little or no earnings to support their market value. Since the first quarter of 2000, a myriad number of internet companies have gone out of business. The reasons for their collapse has been very fundamental. First, many failed internet companies lacked the capital necessary to fund business and expansion from existing operations. Second, there were serious questions about business models. Investors did not want to continue to finance a company with an unproven concept even if it meant passing up a ground floor opportunity to prosper. Stock valuation based upon price/earnings or price/book ratios reached stratospheric levels. These were unsustainable. Since 2000, there has been an industry shakeout that put many internet companies out of business. At this time, choosing industry winners is not difficult. Companies such as Ebay, Yahoo, and Google have carved out lucrative niches within the industry. Factors seem to suggest that companies with a strong content and distribution strategy will be the ultimate survivors.

INVESTING IN THE TECHNOLOGY SECTOR

The technology sector should account for 15 percent of your stock portfolio. The sector provides the highest possible investment return in any given year. However, it is also the highest risk sector. The technology sector suffered dramatically during 2000-2002 period. This substantially lowered the long-term investment returns for this sector. Because technology stocks are so volatile and the opportunity for loss is high, a diversified strategy should be followed. Stock selection within technology should cover a very broad range of sub-sectors.

Nine to eleven stocks should be chosen from this list. Special focus should be on industry leaders. The quickest way to lose money in this sector is to focus on the laggards. In choosing an individual stock from the technology list, consider the following;

- *Choose only those firms that are No #1 or #2 in their respective industries or a particular market segment*

- *Choose companies that have or are developing products or services that represent significant technological advancements or improvements*

- *Select those that have strong fundamentals, strong management, and strong product positioning*

- *Broadly diversify among the various sub-sectors. Do not concentrate your investment in any one sub-sector.*

- *Select companies of a large size (5 billion market cap >).*

- *Attempt to add to your portfolio when technology stocks are out of favor (see Chapter 11).*

- *Stay defensive; never get too excited about this sector. Keep your investments within tight boundaries.*

Table 7.1 *

Technology Stocks	Market Cap
Adobe Systems	6,065
Agilent Technologies	8,261
Alcatel SA ADR A	8,537
Analog Devices	9,016
Applied Materials	22,281
Cisco Systems	102,467
Computer Associates Intl.	8,570
Dell Computer	63,835
EMC	15,091
Ericsson Telephone ADR B	16,134
Hewlett-Packard	37,425
Hitachi ADR	13,118

Table 7.1 (Continued)[*]

IBM	136,069
Infosys Technologies ADR	9,008
Intel	107,921
Intuit	9,931
KLA-Tencor	6,742
Kyocera ADR	10,932
Lexmark International	7,479
Linear Technology	8,365
Lucent Technologies	6,060
Maxim Integrated	10,428
Micron Technology	5,366
Microsoft	274,433
Motorola	20,133
Nextel	31,224
NEC ADR	6,249
Nokia ADR	70,637
Nortel Networks	8,716
Oracle	61,969
Qualcomm	29,017
SAP AG ADR	28,082
Siemens AG ADR	36,630
STMicroelectronics NV	16,881
Sun Microsystems	11,057
Symantec	6,570
Taiwan Semiconductor	27,380

Table 7.1 (Continued)*

Texas Instruments	24,494
Toshiba	9,657
Veritas Software	7,145
Xilinx	7,605

* Table 7.1. Source: Value Line
   Market Cap is presented in millions

8

Energy Sector

"Drill for oil? You mean drill into the ground to try and find oil? You're crazy!"

—Edwin Drake, 1859

The energy sector is composed of 4 major industry groups; integrated oil & gas, oil & gas equipment and service, natural gas producers/utilities, and refining & marketing firms. Oil and natural gas are considered to be "commodities." That is, they are basic materials that are available from a wide variety of suppliers and whose prices are intensely subject to the laws of supply and demand. The prices of virtually all commodities, from copper to pork bellies, had been very low throughout the late 1990s and early 2000s. This has dramatically changed over the past two years as the price of oil has increased above $60 a barrel.

In general, the energy sector today is one of 1) heightened competition, 2) increased capacity and lower operating costs-both driven by dramatic leaps forward in technology, and therefore, 3) restricted supply, typically leading to higher prices. Energy stocks represent a 10.1 percent weighting of the benchmark S&P 500 Index. Historically, the energy sector has delivered a 12.5 percent annual return over the past 29 year period ending December 31st, 2005. Future performance of the energy sector will be determined by global demand and future energy needs.

GLOBAL DEMAND

While ExxonMobil, BP and the other major oil firms are undeniably huge enterprises, the vast majority of oil is still owned by various national governments through their state-owned oil companies. In fact, the governments of such major producers as Mexico, Venezuela, and Saudi Arabia control about 90 percent of the reserves and 69 percent of the production of the world's oil and gas. Consequently, political considerations will continue to be of intense influence on the energy business.

World oil consumption has been increasing at a rate of 2.2 percent per year since 1993, and reached 85.6 million barrels per day in the first quarter of 2005. Although the U.S. currently accounts for ¼ of world consumption, growth in oil use has been lower in the U.S. than in the rest of the world for the last 40 years. The Energy Information Administration (EIA) projects that world oil demand will grow between 1.1 percent and 2.7 percent per year through 2020. Mid-range forecasts of demand growth worldwide are 1.9 percent per year.

Oil consumption in Asian countries will be equal to that in the U.S by 2020. China, India, and South Korea will more than double their oil consumption over this period. Similarly, demand in Central and South America is expected to double. Even the USGS's most optimistic assessment of remaining conventional oil resources, matched with the EIA's Low Economic Growth Case for world oil demand, implies that 50 percent of the world's total endowment of oil will be used up before 2040.

Pessimistic assumptions and high economic growth would put the 50 percent exhaustion point at 2010. Because of the lack of investment in oilfield and natural gas development over the past 15 years, reserves are now at the lowest level since 1979.

SUB-SECTOR ANALYSIS

The integrated oil & gas industry represents 6 percent of the benchmark S&P 500. Major international energy companies engaged in the diverse aspects of oil and gas operations including crude oil & gas exploration, production, manufacturing, refining, marketing & transportation. Major oil companies include international integrated oil companies that are involved in every aspect of the oil business from exploration and production to refining/marketing. Most are busy in the manufacture and sale of petrochemical products. Major companies include ExxonMobil, ConocoPhilips, BP Amoco, Total, and Chevron-Texaco.

The oil & gas equipment and service industry Companies involved in this sub-sector manufacture oil field equipment or provide service to the major international oil firms. Manufacturers produce drill bits, drill rigs, lifts, geophysical prospecting equipment, valves, and wellheads. Servicing companies provide drilling and exploration support by means of offshore and onshore drilling consulting as well as related oil well and contracting services, including seismic surveys, equipment and tool rental, pumping and processing services, inspection and contracting services.

The major issue confronting the industry is the outdated energy infrastructure. This energy space has lacked major new investment for the past 15 years. Investment has been lacking because producers have emphasized return on capital rather than production growth. Production growth is now on the forefront as the major oil companies try to reduce their exposure to the low margin refining business. Therefore, the demand for exploration and drilling activity by major oil and refining companies is due to expand exponentially. Major players include Schlumberger, Halliburton, Global SantaFe, and Transocean.

The natural gas industry breaks into three different types: producers, pipeline companies, and distribution companies. Natural gas burns cleaner than many other traditional fossil fuels and is produced along with oil by drilling into the earth's crust where pockets of gas have been trapped for hundreds of years. Natural gas is delivered by both diversified utilities and LDCs. Diversified utilities that provide natural gas are Duke Energy, Powergen, and Texas Utililties. Major LDCs include AGL Resources and Cascade Natural Gas. LDCs purchase, transport, and resell natural gas to end users such as residential, commercial, industrial gas companies, and electric utilities. Natural gas companies are usually granted exclusive rights to distribute gas to end users in specific geographical locations. The residential market supplies the lion's share of a utilities profits and accounts for the majority of its customers.

Global warming could have a substantial impact upon natural gas companies. Global warming is the process of gas emissions that are warming up the earth's atmosphere. In 1997, 150 nations agreed to reduce the number of dangerous emissions that pollute the environment. This should help increase our reliance on natural gas companies over the next twenty years.

The refining and marketing companies are engaged in downstream activities which includes refining and selling crude oil products such as gasoline, jet fuel, heating oil, motor oil, and lubricants. These companies include Ashland Oil, Quaker State, Tosco Corp., and Ultramar Diamond Shamrock. Marketing is the delivery of products to end users through retail gasoline stations.

INVESTING IN THE ENERGY SECTOR

The energy sector should account for 10 percent of your stock portfolio. The sector provides an excellent balance to the main components of our recommended portfolio; healthcare, financials, and technology.

This is due to the low correlation the energy sector has with the other three recommended sectors, 0.19, 0.45, and 0.02 respectively. Energy stocks also reduce the volatility of your overall stock portfolio due to their low betas. Most of the major international oil companies have betas under 0.70.

Stock selection should consist of five to seven energy stocks, covering the range of the sub-sector. The list below provides you with the major companies within the energy sector. In choosing an individual stock from the energy list, consider the following;

• *Choose only those firms that are No #1 or #2 in their respective industries or a particular market segment.*

• *Ensure that you have exposure to those energy stocks that have a high correlation to the price of oil (oil equipment & service companies and drillers)*

• *Select those firms that have strong fundamentals, strong management, and strong product positioning*

• *Select companies of a large size (5 billion market cap >). Attempt to add to your portfolio when energy stocks are out of favor (see Chapter 11).*

Table 8.1 *

Energy Stocks	Market Cap
Amerada Hess	5,242
Anadarko Petroleum	11,488
Apache Oil	9,991
Baker Hughes	10,668
BHP Billiton	20,884

Table 8.1 (Continued)*

BJ Services	5,611
BP PLC ADR	145,467
Burlington Resources	9,441
ChevronTexaco	64,441
China Petroleum	16,554
ConocoPhillips	74,005
Devon Energy	7,920
EnCana Corp	15,991
Eni S.P.A. ADR	59,796
Exxon Mobil	227,706
GlobalSanteFe	9,833
Halliburton	8,995
Imperial Oil	11,997
Marathon Oil	7,012
Nabors Industries	5,927
Noble Corp	5,045
Petro-Canada	9,459
Petroleo Brasileiro ADR	14,113
Repsol YPF	17,006
Royal Dutch Petroleum	81,526
Schlumberger	36,113
Shell Transport	54,883
Statoil ASA	16,404
Suncor Energy	8,114
Talisman Energy	5,440

Table 8.1 (Continued)*

TOTAL ADR	87,347
Transocean	16,440
Weatherford International	5,502
YPF S.A.	6,222

* Table 8.1. Source: Value Line
  Market Cap is presented in millions

9
REIT's & Bonds

"Good intelligence is nine-tenths of any battle."

—Napolean

In addition to common stocks, income instruments, such as Real Estate Investment Trusts (REIT's) and bonds, are an essential part of an investment portfolio. I recommend these investments as a complement to a diversified portfolio. A REIT is a company that buys, develops, manages, and sells real estate assets. REIT's are actually considered an equity product, or stock. However, in this text I list them under the income component category. This is due to their high dividends or yield, and their unique relationship with equities. REITs basically allow participants to invest in a professionally-managed portfolio of real estate properties. Typically, REITs concentrate in one type: apartments, offices, shopping malls, hotels, and even storage units.

The attraction for investors is two-fold. First, REITs offer a chance to own a diversified piece of choice properties that could appreciate in value—especially if inflation returns. And second, these companies are required by law to pay out 90 percent of the rents they collect in the form of dividends to shareholders. Therefore, many REITs have dividend yields of 5 percent or more, which is very attractive in today's investment environment. REITs qualify as pass-through entities, companies who are able to distribute the majority of income cash flows to investors without taxation at the corporate level. As pass-through entities, whose main function is to pass profits on to investors, a REIT's business activities are generally restricted to generation of property rental income.

A major advantage of a REIT investment instead of traditional private ownership is its liquidity (ease of liquidation of assets into cash). One reason for the liquid nature of REIT investments is that its shares are primarily traded on major stock exchanges, making it very easy to buy and sell REIT assets/shares than to buy and sell properties in private markets. More than 180 REITs are publicly traded, with market capitalization topping $170 billion. In considering REITs as an alternative investment choice, an investor should examine two important criteria. One, they must provide above average investment returns over time. Two, they must provide diversification benefits to an overall portfolio. Fortunately, REITs provide both qualities.

The compound overall return of REITs is attractive. According to data provided by William Bernstein, REIT stocks have registered a compound annual total return of 16.8 percent from 1976 through 2005. The returns have been extremely attractive over the past five years, as interest rates have declined. A major portion of the REIT return comes from the high dividend yields. The average REIT that trades on the New York Stock Exchange paid out a 5.2 percent yield in the form of a cash dividend in 2004. Equally important, their performance has differed significantly from the other major asset classes; especially large-company stocks and bonds. Ibbotson found that the correlation (Chapter 2) of REIT stock returns with the returns of other common stocks is quite low. More importantly, the correlation has consistenly declined over the past 30-year time frame.

Over the past seven years, the correlation with the S&P 500 declined 61 percent, from .64 to .25. The correlation of REIT returns with those of U.S. long-term bonds declined 41 percent, from .27 to .16 during the same span. These correlations are extremely low and provide outstanding diversification benefits. Many pundits argue that investing in REITs is quite similar to investing in small company stocks. However, the data dispels this myth. Over the past seven years, the correlation to small company stocks also declined a distinguished 65 percent, from .74 to .26. There are several reasons for the low level of correlation. Many real estate lease agreements are entered into for years at a time, so rentals continue without regard to short-term economic swings. As a result, real estate values appear to lag the economic market cycle. In addition, because sales are infrequent, many institutional investors rely on appraisals to value a REIT. These appraisals appear to smooth the market value of the properties, understating volatility.

In addition to low correlation, REITs also possess low relative historical volatility (beta) and provide some degree of inflation protection. REITs are generally stable. This is primarily due to their high dividend yields and asset backed equity. The recent behavior of REITs as an asset class makes for a strong case for their inclusion in portfolios as a hedge against the volatility and underperformance of other securities. For example, a recent study demonstrated that adding a minimum 10 percent REITs to a portfolio boosted the average annual return by almost half a percentage point over the non-REIT portfolio, while reducing portfolio risk by that same amount. The study, done by Ibbotson, authenticated that a $10,000 investment in the non-REIT portfolio in 1972 with dividends reinvested would have grown to $219,049 by 2004. A second portfolio, including a 10 percent REIT allocation, would have gained $227,000 over the same period. And the third portfolio, which included 20 percent REITs, would have accumulated $238,349, an increase of more than $19,000 over the non-REIT portfolio. In short, a lower-risk (more diversified) portfolio beat a higher risk portfolio hands down.

BONDS: ARE THEY WORTH IT

It was not long ago that bonds seemed a dull and depressing choice compared to the smashing returns offered by stocks. After all, bonds are confusing, arcane, and downright dowdy when it comes to other investments. While stocks have averaged just over 11 percent annual growth over the last 50 years, long-term government bonds have slogged along at 6.6 percent. But bonds provide a safety net from stocks. While stocks fell hard throughout the early part of this decade, U.S. Treasury Bonds rose—as they often do in times of turmoil on Wall Street. And in the end, more than a few aggressive equity investors have learned the hard way why diversification counts.

When stocks are in decline, even a 7 percent gain elsewhere in your portfolio can do a lot to ease the pain. From March 2000 to December 2003, long-term U.S. government bonds returned a cumulative 35.8 percent. A solid dose of bonds would thus have substantially eased the pain of the equity portion of your portfolio. During the 2000-2002 bear market, a portfolio consisting of stocks alone dropped twice as much as a portfolio with a mix of stocks and bonds. The lesson is clear: Unless you have substantial time to make up for short-term losses in the stock market, you would be silly not to diversify your portfolio with at least *some* exposure to bonds. But too much bonds can result in another problem; inflation-adjusted returns. Since inflation has averaged almost 4 percent over the past 50 years, bonds actually provide only a small amount of what is called real return.

Real return is defined as the return of the investment minus inflation. If the inflation rate is 3 percent in a year that your investment provides an 8 percent return, your real return after correcting for inflation, is 5 percent. The greater your real return, the larger your account value grows. Real return is the primary reason that emphasizing capital preservation to the exclusion of growth can leave you short financially over the long term. That's because your return on the most conservative investments rarely exceeds the rate of inflation by two percentage points—and is frequently less. If you're earning 1.75 percent on an insured money market account when inflation is 2 percent, you have a negative real return of 0.25 percent. Some other statistics:

- A dollar invested in Treasury bills between 1928 and 2001 earned a 3.8 percent average annual return. Yet, according to the U.S. Consumer Price Index, inflation during that same period averaged 3.3 percent. The T-bills' real return? Only 0.6 percent.

- A dollar invested in long-term U.S. government and corporate bonds over the same period earned a 5.8 percent average annual return. Less inflation, the real return is 2.5 percent. Better than T-bills, but not by much.

- A dollar invested in U.S. common stocks over this period generated an 11.4 percent average annual return. The real return: 8.1 percent. That is three times better than bonds and head and shoulders above T-bills.

The only investment that provides immunity to a negative or low real return is stocks. So what is the bottom line? A small portion of bonds is always sensible, even for the most aggressive investor. I generally recommend about a 15 percent to 35 percent weighting in bonds depending on your risk tolerance and investment horizon. However, even for the most conservative investor, I recommend no more than 35 percent be allocated to bonds. In Chapter 14, I examine the overall returns of several model portfolios containing no more than 35 percent bonds.

BONDS: WHICH ONES?

Now that I have convinced you a sensible investing approach includes bonds, we turn to which bonds are best. Although there are several different categories of bonds, let's examine the four most popular I.O.U.s.

CATEGORY	RETURN	CORRELATION TO S&P 500
U.S. Treasury 5-Yr	8.82%	0.18
U.S. Treasury 30-Yr	8.72%	0.36
U.S. Corporate Bonds	9.33%	0.52
International Bonds	9.44%	0.07

Table 9.1 Source: Ibbotson, 1973-2005

In table 9.1, international bonds possess the highest investment return of any bond category. Remarkably, they are generally not in the average investor's portfolio. Most investors seem to think that these bonds are quite risky. In reality, they are not. These bonds provide great diversification to a stock portfolio. They are especially attractive when the U.S. economy is floundering and the dollar is losing value against international currencies. Currency changes play a major part in the diversification benefits of international bonds. The returns from international bonds come not only from the bonds themselves but also from currency fluctuations.

The idea behind this currency effect is when the U.S. dollar is weak, your returns are enhanced. This is because when you sell an international bond and convert the foreign currency back into U.S. dollars, you can buy more dollars. These extra dollars can significantly add to your overall return. International bonds are as varied as U.S. bonds. You can buy foreign government or corporate bonds, or a mix of them, from just about any country. Buying individual international bonds is not an easy process. In fact, some brokers cannot even provide the service for you or will charge hefty fees. I recommend that you do not attempt buying international bonds unless you possess a large sum of money (generally $500,000 or above) and have a reliable broker that is familiar with these type of bonds. The best method for a small investor is to buy international bonds through a fund.

A major concern with funds is that many of them hedge their portfolios. Hedging is an additional expense the fund incurs to get rid of fluctuations caused by changes in the relative currency rates. But, it is those fluctuations that make international bonds such a great investment. I recommend you only utilize a fund that does not hedge its portfolio. There are several recommendations of un-hedged international bond funds in Chapter 14. Outside of international bonds, 5-Year Treasury Notes offer the most compelling diversification benefits. Although the returns of corporate bonds are more attractive, the correlation of corporate bonds and stocks is quite high. Therefore, a combination of international bonds and intermediate U.S. Treasuries is the most sensible choice. Both offer the best diversification with a portfolio composed primarily of stocks.

10
Fundamental Analysis

"Great intellects are skeptical"

—Nietzsche

Fundamental analysis involves the use of financial and economic data to evaluate a company. Notice that the title of this chapter is not "stock analysis." Though evaluating a stock is the most common phrase utilized when performing research, your focus should be on evaluating a business. Before ever buying stock, you must access the fundamental condition of the business itself. If the business passes several key tests, then you can examine the stock to determine if it is reasonably valued.

The future of each share of company stock is always tied inextricably to the fortune of the underlying business, and the market's perception of the future prospects for that business. As an astute analyst, you must basically answer three key questions;

1. Is this a financially sound company?

2. Is this company a financial leader in its respective industry?

3. Is the company's stock priced attractively right now?

If the answer to all three questions is yes, then you have identified an engaging stock candidate. You start the process by evaluating the liquidity, solvency, efficiency and, most importantly, the earnings potential of a given company. To determine this, you will depend on a financial analyst's toolkit, which includes the corporation's annual report, 10K and 10Q, independent analyst's research reports, and macro-economic data. With this information in hand, your goal is to thoroughly examine a company and ultimately resolve the above three questions. This is not an easy process. While it is not critical for the average investor to fully understand every aspect of financial statement analysis, it is necessary to have a broad understanding of what goes within a companies' financial statements. Investors who can perform good fundamental analysis and spot pricing discrepancies will be able to build a portfolio of superlative stocks.

Before we begin evaluating the different approaches to common stock evaluation, a quick review of a firm's primary financial statements is needed. There are two major financial statements that an investor must review before undertaking the task of stock evaluation.

1. *The Balance Sheet*

2. *The Income Statement*

This section is designed to teach you some basic methods for analyzing both the balance sheet and income statement. Analyzing both statements is an important tool to help investors appraise their investment options.

BALANCE SHEET ANALYSIS

The analysis of a balance sheet is done to identify potential liquidity problems. These may signify the company's inability to meet financial obligations. An investor also can examine the degree to which a company is leveraged, or indebted. An overly leveraged company may have difficulties raising future capital. Even more severe, they may be headed towards bankruptcy. These are just a few of the danger signs that can be detected with careful analysis of a balance sheet.

As an investor, you will want to know if a company you are considering is in danger of not being able to make its payments. After all, some of the company's obligations will be to you if you choose to invest in it. To find out, you should turn to several of the most fundamental financial ratios. The first is the current ratio. The current ratio measures a firm's ability to pay their current obligations. The greater the extent to which current assets exceed current liabilities, the easier a company can meet its short-term obligations.

$$\textbf{Current Ratio} = \frac{\text{Current Assets}}{\text{Current Liabilities}}$$

After calculating the current ratio for a company, you should compare it with other companies in the same industry. A ratio lower than that of the industry average suggests that the company may have liquidity problems. Most accountants claim that a ratio of 2.0 (twice as many current assets as current liabilities) is a good benchmark, but it depends on the business. High-growth companies need a larger cushion to finance rapid expansion, while big, established firms can get away with less. Attention should also be paid to the current ratio trend over time. A low, but stable current ratio is less of a problem than a sharply declining ratio that might signal either unsustainable growth or a deteriorating business. Both conditions are serious red flags for any investor.

The quick ratio (also known as acid test) is very similar to the current ratio except for the fact that it excludes inventory. For this reason, it is also a more conservative ratio.

$$\textbf{Quick Ratio} = \frac{\text{Current Assets—Inventory}}{\text{Current Liabilities}}$$

Inventory is excluded in this ratio because, in many industries, inventory cannot be quickly converted to cash. Sometimes, the value of the inventory is inflated or perhaps even worthless. If this is the case, inventory should not be included as an asset that can be used to pay off short-term obligations. Like the current ratio, to have a quick ratio at or above the industry average is desirable. A quick ratio over 1 shows proper liquidity. Working capital is an additional measure of liquidity. It is the amount that current assets exceed current liabilities. Here it is in the form of an equation:

Working Capital =   Current Assets—Current Liabilities

This formula is very similar to the current ratio. The only difference is it gives you a dollar amount rather than a ratio. It is calculated to determine a firm's ability to pay its short-term obligations. Positive working capital can be viewed as somewhat of a security blanket. The greater the amount of working capital, the more security an investor can have that the firm will be able to meet financial obligations.

Another critical element of a firm's financial condition is its debt characteristics. The long-term debt to equity ratio measures a company's capital structure. In other words, it measures how a company finances its assets on a long-term basis.

LT Debt to Equity Ratio = $\dfrac{\text{Long-Term Debt}}{\text{Total Equity}}$

A firm that finances its assets with a high percentage of debt is potentially risking bankruptcy. This may happen if the economy struggles or the business does not perform as well as expected. A firm with a lower percentage of debt has a bigger safety cushion should times turn bad. A related side effect of being highly leveraged is the unwillingness of lenders to provide more debt financing. In this case, a firm that finds itself in a jam may have to issue stock on unfavorable terms. All in all, being highly leveraged is generally viewed as disadvantageous due to the increased risk of bankruptcy, higher borrowing costs, and decreased financial flexibility. On the other hand, using debt financing does have advantages. Stockholder's potential return on their investment is greater when a firm borrows more. Borrowing also has some tax advantages. Overall, a company that is highly leveraged adds another layer of risk for a stockholder.

INCOME STATEMENT ANALYSIS

The income statement is important for investors because it is the basic measuring stick of profitability. A company with little or no income has little chance of future growth or money to pass on to its investors in the form of dividends. If a company continues to record losses for a sustained period, it could easily go bankrupt. By analyzing an income statement properly, you can begin to evaluate the effectiveness of the management on the operations of the firm. Proper income sheet analysis can help identify worthy investment opportunities. It can also reduce the risk involved with choosing a poor investment. Assuming the firm checks out for reasonable financial soundness in the balance sheet analysis, you may then turn your attention to the bottom line of the income statement earnings per share. This figure represents the total net income divided by the number of shares the firm has issued.

$$\text{E.P.S.} = \frac{\text{Net Income}}{\text{\# of shares outstanding}}$$

Think of E.P.S. as your share of the corporation's overall profit if it paid everything out to the stockholders and kept nothing to reinvest in the business. If the earnings are declining over time or jump around unpredictably, then the company in question can have serious problems. Many industries, such as autos or airlines, are subject to the business cycle and have dramatic swings in earnings per share. The more stable a firm's E.P.S. is over time, the less overall risk you assume as an investor.

Few things will panic investors more than a company that is unable to make its interest payments. That is why it is critical to ensure that the firm can meet the demands of its creditors even during a temporary downturn. A method to calculate these demands is the interest coverage ratio. It takes the earnings before interest and taxes, or EBIT and divides it by the interest expense to figure out how many times over the interest payments could be met with current income. It gives you a sense of how far a company's earnings can fall before it will start defaulting on its bond payments.

Interest Coverage = $\dfrac{\text{Earnings Before Interest \& Taxes}}{\text{Interest Payments}}$

Look for companies that are able to cover their interest charges at least three to four times over. As a general rule of thumb, investors should not own a stock that has an interest coverage ratio under 2. An interest coverage ratio below 1.0 indicates the business is having difficulties generating the cash necessary to pay its interest obligations. The history and consistency of earnings is tremendously important. The more consistent a company's earnings, the lower the acceptable interest coverage ratio can be. The higher this ratio, the more safety built into the stock.

Next you should examine profit margins. There are several different ratios to research; gross profit margin, operating profit margin, and net profit margin. Profitability is often measured in percentage terms in order to facilitate making comparisons of a company's financial performance against past year's performance and against the performance of other companies. When profitability is expressed as a percentage (or ratio), the new figures are called profit margins. The most common profit margins are all expressed as percentages of net sales. Lets look at a few of the most commonly used profit margins you can easily learn to use to help you measure and compare firms:

Gross Profit Margin = $\dfrac{\text{Gross Profit}}{\text{Total Sales}}$

Since this ratio only takes into account sales and variable costs (costs of goods sold), this ratio is a good indicator of a firm's efficiency in producing and distributing its products. A firm with a ratio superior to the industry average demonstrates superior efficiency in its production processes. The higher the ratio, the higher the efficiency of the production process. Within certain industries, the gross margin is not relevant. This is because many companies do not have a cost of goods sold line. As the name implies, operating margin is the resulting ratio when operating income is divided by net sales.

$$\textbf{Operating Profit Margin} = \frac{\text{Operating Profit}}{\text{Total Sales}}$$

This ratio measures the quality of a firm's operations. A firm with a high operating margin in relation to the industry average has operations that are more efficient. Typically, to achieve this result, the company must have lower fixed costs, a better gross margin, or a combination of the two. At any rate, companies that are more efficient than their competitors in their core operations have a distinct advantage. The last profitability measure we will cover in this section is net margin. As the name implies, net margin is a measure of profitability for the sum of a firm's operations.

$$\textbf{Net Profit Margin} = \frac{\text{Net Profit}}{\text{Total Sales}}$$

As with the other ratios you will want to compare net margin with that of other companies in the industry. You can also track year-to-year changes in net margin to see if a company's competitive position is improving or getting worse. The higher the net margin relative to the industry (or relative to past years), the better. Often a high net margin indicates that the company you are looking at is an efficient producer with a dominant position in its industry. However, as with all the previous profit margin measurements, you need to always check past years of performance. You want to make sure that good results are not a fluke. Strong profit margins that are sustainable indicate that a company has been able to consistently outperform its competitors. The savvy investor uses profitability margins to help analyze income statements of prospective investments. Companies with high interest coverage ratios, gross margins, operating margins, and net margins will always be very attractive to investors.

Once you have completed the balance sheet and income statement analysis, your attention should be focused on six key financial valuation statistics;

Price/Earnings Ratio

Chances are you have heard the term P/E ratio used before. The price/earnings ratio is one of the oldest and most frequently used metrics when it comes to valuing stocks. This is the earnings per share divided by the average primary shares outstanding over the last twelve months.

Price/Earnings =   Price of Share of Stock
                            E.P.S.

The P/E ratio gives you an indication of a stock's value. If it is low (though some sectors tend to be chronically low) it usually means that the stock price reflects a reasonable valuation relative to the earnings stream. If it is high (though some sectors tend to be chronically high) it usually means that the stock price reflects a high valuation relative to the earnings stream. The majority of the time the P/E is calculated using EPS from the last four quarters. This is also known as the trailing P/E. However, it can also be utilized by estimating the E.P.S. figure expected over the next four quarters. This is known as the leading or forward P/E. A third variation is also sometimes used that consists of the past two quarters and estimates of the next two quarters. There is not a huge difference between these variations. It is important you realize that you are using actual historical data for the calculation in the first case. The other two are based on analyst estimates that are not always perfect or precise.

The P/E ratio is a much better indicator of the value of a stock than the market price alone. For example, all things being equal, a $10 stock with a P/E of 75 is much more expensive than a $100 stock with a P/E of 20. Therefore, the P/E ratio allows you to compare two different companies with two different market prices—comparing "apples" to "apples", so to speak. A potential problem with the P/E involves companies that are not profitable and consequently have a negative E.P.S. There are varying opinions on how to deal with this. I recommend that if a firm does not have a P/E due to depressed earnings, an investor should use an alternative valuation model, such as the Price/Sales ratio. Its difficult to state whether a particular P/E is high or low without taking into account two main factors:

1. *Company growth rates*—A P/E is primarily based upon the growth rate of the prospective company. Generally, the higher the growth rate, the higher the expected P/E. If the projected growth rate does not justify the P/E, then a stock might be overpriced.

2. *Industry*—Comparing P/E ratios of companies is much more beneficial if they are in the same industry. For example, auto companies typically have low P/E ratios because they possess low earnings growth. In contrast, the technology industry is characterized by high growth rates. Comparing an auto firm to a technology stalwart is fruitless. You should concentrate on comparing companies to their competition. This is known as relative valuation.

Historically, the average P/E ratio in the market has been around 15. This fluctuates significantly depending on economic conditions at the time. Periods of high inflation are generally marked with low P/E ratios. Vice versa, periods of low inflation are signified by high P/E ratios.

Price/Sales Ratio

This ratio is the total revenue (sales) divided by the average primary shares outstanding over the last twelve months. It also gives an indication of value. If it is low it usually means that the stock price reflects a reasonable valuation relative to the revenue stream. If it is high it usually means that the stock price reflects a high valuation relative to the revenue stream. I recommend the P/S ratio as an alternative valuation tool, especially when a firm has no P/E ratio.

Price/Sales =   Price of Share of Stock
                      Sales Per Share

PEG Ratio

The relationship between the price/earnings ratio and earnings growth tells a much more complete story than the P/E on its own. This is called the PEG Ratio. It is formulated as:

PEG Ratio =   P/E Ratio
                    Annual Expected 5-yr E.P.S. Growth

The PEG ratio compares a stock's price/earnings (P/E) ratio to its expected E.P.S growth rate. I utilize the expected growth rate over the next five years as the denominator. Of course, predicting the five-year growth rate is quite difficult. It is an inexact science. Generally, an assumed five-year growth rate is based both upon the past growth and the future potential of the firm. If the PEG ratio is equal to one, it means that the market is pricing the stock to fully reflect the stock's E.P.S growth. If the PEG ratio is greater than one, it indicates that the stock is evaluated above its growth rate or possibly that the market anticipates future EPS growth to be superior. If the PEG ratio is less than one, it is a sign of a possibly undervalued stock or that the market does not expect the company to achieve the earnings growth that is reflected in the Wall Street estimates. It is important to note that the PEG ratio cannot be used in isolation. Like all financial ratios, to properly use PEG ratios, investors must compare PEG ratios among companies in the same industry. The firms with the highest PEG ratios are ordinarily the market leaders. Ranking industries by their PEG or P/E ratios creates a so called totem pole; where each company falls into place based upon its future outlook.

Amazingly, the PEG ratio for the S&P 500 stock index currently stands at 1.75. Therefore, investors are willing to pay $1.75 for every $1.00 in potential earnings. You should look for investment candidates that possess low PEG ratios

Return on Assets

$$R.O.A = \frac{\text{Net Income}}{\text{Average Total Assets}}$$

R.O.A. is calculated by the profit generated per sales dollar times the sales generated per dollar of assets. This is a measure of how well the company deploys the assets it has. It may have a small asset base from which it generates big revenues. This would be a successful operation. If, however, the company needs added assets to profit, it may need to reassess the business. Return on assets measures a company's earnings in relation to all of the resources it has at its disposal [the shareholders' capital plus short and long-term borrowed funds]. Thus, it is the most stringent and excessive test of return to shareholders.

The lower the profit per dollar of assets, the more asset-intensive a business is. The higher the profit per dollar of assets, the less asset-intensive a business is. All things being equal, the more asset-intensive a business, the more money must be reinvested into it to continue generating earnings. If a company has a R.O.A. of 20 percent, it means that the company earned $0.20 for each $1 in assets. As a general rule, anything below 5 percent is very asset-heavy (manufacturing, railroads, e.g.). Anything above 20 percent is asset-light (advertising firms, software companies, e.g.). As with all other financial ratios, it is critical to examine the R.O.A. of companies within the same industry.

Return on Equity

$$R.O.E. = \frac{Net\ Income}{Shareholder\ Equity}$$

The available common stock income after all expenses, excluding common stock dividends, divided by the average common stock equity (also called the net worth). This is expressed as a percentage and is a measure of how effectively a company's earnings stream is being deployed. R.O.E. is one of the most important profitability metrics. Return on equity reveals how much profit a company earned in comparison to the total amount of shareholder equity found on the balance sheet. A business that has a high return on equity is more likely to be capable of generating significant cash internally. For the most part, the higher a company's return on equity compared to its industry, the better. For most of the twentieth century, the S&P 500 stock index averaged R.O.E.'s of 10 to 15 percent. In the 1990s, the average return on equity was in excess of 20 percent. Of course, this was an anomaly. Expect the average R.O.E. to return to the long-term averages. All other things being equal, a higher number denotes better use of funds.

Free Cash Flow Yield Ratio

$$F.C.F.Y. = \frac{Free\ Cash\ Flow\ Per\ Share}{Price\ of\ Share}$$

This ratio examines a firm's ability to generate cash earnings. It is computed in two steps. First, by taking the trailing twelve month free cash flow divided by the trailing twelve month average number of shares outstanding. Second, by taking this result and dividing it by the current stock price. The reason you should differentiate free cash flow from regular earnings is because companies have non-earnings items like depletion allowances, depreciation credits, interest accrued but not yet paid, tax overpayments, and so on. Free cash flow speaks to the actual dollars a company generates after capital expenditures. It measures the company's true ability to pay its bills and its dividends. This ratio is one of my favorites. It examines what investment return you would earn if you owned every share of outstanding stock, and all cash earnings were paid out to you. If a company generates a 1 percent F.C.F. yield, would you buy out the company? Hopefully, your answer is no. Therefore, you should also avoid the stock.

By applying minimum standards on a F.C.F. yield, you will avoid buying businesses that are extremely overvalued. All of the internet stocks of the late 1990s had either scant or negative F.C.F. yields. Why did their stocks continue to go up? Investors simply did not value these companies properly. They were simply caught up in the hype. Once the hype ran out, these stocks came back to earth, or in many cases ventured into bankruptcy. Any stock you consider should have a F.C.F. yield higher than that of a bond. This recommendation is just common sense. Since you incur added risk by purchasing a stock over a bond, with no guarantee of ever getting your money back, this requirement will at least keep you from taking too much of a gamble with your hard earned cash.

VALUATION APPROACHES

There are basically two different approaches for common stock valuation; top-down and bottom-up. Under either of the two fundamental approaches, an investor will have to work with individual company data. In reality, each of these approaches is used by investors and security analysts when doing fundamental analysis. With the bottom-up approach, investors focus directly on a company's prospects. Analysis of such information as the company's products, its competitive position, and its financial status leads to an estimate of the company's earnings potential, and, ultimately, its value in the market. Considerable time and effort are required to produce the type of detailed financial analysis needed to understand a firm's standing. The emphasis in this approach is on finding companies with good long-term growth prospects, and making accurate earnings estimates.

The top-down approach is the opposite of the bottom-up approach. Investors begin with the economy and the overall market, considering such important factors as interest rates and inflation. They next consider likely industry prospects, or sectors of the economy that are likely to do particularly well (or particularly poorly). Finally, having decided that factors are favorable for investing, and having determined which parts of the overall economy are likely to perform well, individual companies are analyzed.

I believe that both approaches add value. However, since our recommendation is that investors primarily concentrate on four sectors of the economy, a top-down approach is less relevant. Therefore, this chapter will concentrate on the bottoms-up approach. To organize this effort, bottom-up fundamental research is often broken into two categories; growth investing and value investing.

Growth Stocks—Catching the Momentum

The growth style of investing focuses on companies with strong earnings and accelerating capital growth. A growth investor will make investment decisions based on forecasts of continuing growth in earnings. Growth investing emphasizes qualitative criteria, including value judgments about the company, its markets, its management, and its ability to extract future earnings growth from the particular industry. Quantitative indicators of interest to the growth investor include high Price/Earnings ratios, Price/Sales ratios, and low dividend yields.

A high P/E ratio suggests that the market is prepared to pay more per share in anticipation of future earnings. A low dividend yield suggests that the company is reinvesting rather than distributing profits. These indicators are considered in relation to the company's immediate competitors. The companies with the highest P/E ratios relative to their industry will often be dominant within their market segment and have strong growth prospects. Growth investors will generally focus on premium and leading-edge companies.

Some industry sectors by their nature have stronger growth characteristics, particularly more innovative and speculative industries. For example, during the bull run on the U.S. stock markets during the late 1990s, the technology sector was a major area of growth investment. On observing strong earnings growth, a growth investor will decide whether to buy shares based on whether the company's growth is going to continue at its present rate, to increase, or to decrease. If it is expected to increase, the growth investor will consider it a candidate for purchase.

The key research question is: at what point will the company's growth flatten out, or fall? If a company's growth rate slows or reverses, it is no longer attractive to a growth investor. Growth investors are normally prepared to pay a premium for what they believe to be high quality shares. The potential downside in growth investing is that if a company goes into sudden decline and the share price falls, you can lose capital value rapidly.

Growth stocks carry high expectations of above-average future growth in earnings and above-average valuations. Investors expect these stocks to perform well in the future and are willing to pay high P/E multiples for this expected growth. The danger is that the price may become too high. Generally, once a company sports a P/E ratio above 50, the risk significantly escalates. Many technology growth stocks traded at a P/E ratio of above 100 during 1999. This is unsustainable. No company in the history of the stock market has been able to maintain such a high P/E level for a sustained period of time.

Value Stocks—Looking for Bargains

The bargain-hunting value style is looking for shares that are underpriced in relation to the company's future potential. A value investor will invest in a company in the expectation that its shares will increase in value over time. Value investing is based essentially on quantitative criteria; asset values, cash flow, and discounted future earnings. The key properties of value shares are low Price/Earnings, Price/Sales ratios, and normally higher dividend yields.

On observing a company's earnings growth, a value manager will decide whether to buy shares based on the company's consistency or recovery prospects. The key research questions are: 1) Does the current P/E ratio warrant an investment in a slow growth company or 2) Is the company a higher growth candidate that has dropped in price due to a temporary problem. If this is the case, will the company's earnings growth recover, and if so, when? The key to value investing is to find bargain shares (priced low historically or for temporary and/or irrational reasons), avoiding shares that are merely cheap (priced low because the company is failing).

The buying opportunity is identified when a company undergoing some immediate problems is perceived to have good chances of recovery in the medium to long term. If there is a loss in market confidence in the company, the share price may fall, and the value investor can step in. Once the share price has achieved a suitable value, reflecting the predicted turnaround in company performance, the shareholding is sold, realizing a capital gain. A potential risk in value investing is that the company may not turn around, in which case the share price may stay static or fall.

Performance of Growth & Value Stocks

Although many academics argue that value stocks outperform growth stocks, the returns for individuals investing through mutual funds demonstrate a near match. A 2005 study *Do Investors Capture the Value Premium?* written by Todd Houge at The University of Iowa and Tim Loughran at The University of Notre Dame found that large company mutual funds in both the value and growth styles returned just over 11 percent for the period of 1975 to 2002. This paper contradicted many studies that demonstrated owning value stocks offers better long-term performance than growth stocks. These studies, led by Eugene Fama and Kenneth French, established the current consensus that the value style of investing does indeed offer a return premium. There are several theories as to why this has been the case, among the most persuasive being a series of behavioral arguments put forth by leading researchers. These studies suggest that the outperformance of value stocks may result from investors' tendency toward common behavioral traits, including the belief that the future will be similar to the past, overreaction to unexpected events, "herding" behavior which leads at times to overemphasis of a particular style or sector, overconfidence, and aversion to regret. All of these behaviors can cause price anomalies which create buying opportunities for value investors.

Another key ingredient argued for value outperformance is lower business appraisals. Value stocks are plainly confined to a P/E range, whereas growth stocks have an upper limit that is infinite. When growth stocks reach a high plateau in regard to P/E ratios, the ensuing returns are generally much lower than the category average over time. In addition, growth stocks tend to lose more in bear markets. In the last two major bear markets, growth stocks fared far worse than value. From January 1973 until late 1974, large growth stocks lost 45 percent of their value, while lage value stocks lost 26 percent. Similarly, from April 2000 to September 2002, large growth stocks lost 46 percent versus only 27 percent for large value stocks. These losses, academics insist, dramatically reduce the long-term investment returns of growth stocks.

However, the recent study by Houge and Loughran reasoned that although a premium may exist, investors have not been able to capture the excess return through mutual funds. The study also maintained that any potential value premium is generated outside the securities held by most mutual funds. Simply put, being growth or value had no material impact on a mutual fund's performance. Listed below in Table 10.1 are the annualized returns and standard deviations for return data from January 1975 through December 2005:

Index	Return	SD
S&P 500	11.53%	14.88%
Large Growth Funds	11.30%	16.65%
Large Value Funds	11.41%	15.39%

* *Table 10.1 Source: Hough/Loughran Study*

The Hough/Loughran study also found that the returns by style also varied over time. From 1965-1983, a period widely known to favor the value style, large value funds averaged a 9.92 percent annual return, compared to 8.73 percent for large growth funds. This performance differential reverses over 1984-2001, as large growth funds generated a 14.1 percent average return compared to 12.9 percent for large value funds. Thus, one style can outperform in any time period. However, although the long-term returns are nearly identical, large differences between value and growth returns happen over time. This is especially the case over the last ten years as growth and value have had extraordinary return differences—sometimes over *30 percentage points* of underperformance. Table 10.2 below indicates the return differential between the value and growth styles since 1992.

Year	Growth	Value
1992	5.1%	**10.5%**
1993	1.7%	**18.6%**
1994	**3.1%**	-0.6%
1995	**38.1%**	37.1%
1996	**24.0%**	22.0%
1997	**36.5%**	30.6%
1998	**42.2%**	14.7%
1999	**28.2%**	3.2%
2000	-22.1%	**6.1%**
2001	-26.7%	**7.1%**
2002	-25.2%	**-20.5%**
2003	**28.2%**	27.7%
2004	6.3%	**16.5%**
2005	3.6%	**6.1%**

Table 10.2 Source: Barra Associates

Between the third quarter of 1994 and the second quarter of 2000, the S&P Growth Index produced annualized total returns of 30 percent, versus only about 18 percent for the S&P Value Index. Since 2000, value has turned the tables and dramatically outperformed growth.

Due to the fact that both styles have near equal performance and either style can outperform for a significant time period, I recommend a blending of styles. Rather than attempt to second-guess the market by switching in and out of styles as they roll with the cycle, it is prudent to maintain an equal balance your investment between the two. Fortunately, my recommended sectors; healthcare, financials, technology, and energy offer both value and growth candidates. This is by design. A portfolio composed of stocks from these four sectors will naturally be well diversified between the two unique investment styles.

U.S. Sector Concentration :

	Value	Growth
Capital Equipment	49	51
Consumer Goods	11	89
Energy	**94**	**6**
Finance	**90**	**10**
Healthcare	**35**	**65**
Materials	65	35
Services	41	59
Technology	**8**	**92**

Table 10.3 Source: HSBC, Number of stocks in Value/Growth portfolio as a percentage of the total number of stocks within that sector.

As the table above demonstrates, the technology and healthcare sectors are primarily in the growth category; whereas the financial and energy sectors primarily fall into the value camp.

INTRINSIC & RELATIVE VALUATION

There is further bifurcation with the valuation process. Two additional methods to evaluating the stock price of a company exist; absolute valuation and relative valuation. Absolute valuation models, such as the dividend discount or discounted cash flow models, rely upon data from the given firm and then a forecast of future streams of earnings, dividends, or cash. In regard to absolute models, the discounted cash-flow method is the most popular. Money managers and academics have been using it for decades, coming up with numerous variations: the dividend-discount model (best suited for companies paying dividends) and the discounted-cash-flow-to-the-firm model (DCF) being the most popular. Investment bankers also use these models to price companies involved in mergers or acquisitions.

These models, with their various permutations, are all an attempt to do the same two things: First, look at factors such as growth rates and profit margins to project how much money a company can generate in the future. Second, discount the future cash flows back to today's dollars. The difficulty in these models is the substantial differences that result by only making small changes in the inputs. While this method is philosophically correct, it is a very impractical model. Therefore, I recommend a relative value approach to stock valuation.

Relative valuation models utilize the previously mentioned ratios, such as P/E, P/S, PEG, etc. Relative value seeks to determine the true value of a stock by comparing these multiples to those of the overall market, similar firms, or the company's own history. For example, if two companies participate in the same industry, with comparable balance sheets and income statements, and equal growth rates, then their P/Es should be very similar. If their P/Es are different, then an analyst must investigate why such a discrepancy exists. If no valid explanation can be found, then it could be considered a good relative value candidate. Each company also has a trading history. Stocks will trade either below, equal to, or above their own historical valuation. Finding stocks that trade at a low historical valuation can offer an investor substantial rewards. In the next chapter, case studies of the relative value technique are fully discussed.

11

Stock Selection

"Do not hire a man who does your work for money, but him who does it for the love of it"

—Henry David Thoreau

To be a successful stock investor, an individual must follow a disciplined approach. There are literally thousands of publicly traded companies. No investor can examine them all. Fortunately, by focusing on the four major sectors of the economy, the list of potential investments is dramatically reduced. In fact, I recommend that you limit your buy list to about 500 publicly traded companies (see end of sector chapters). Within these 500 firms, you will find plenty of attractive candidates. As discussed at the end of Chapters 5, 6, 7, and 8, the following criteria should be utilized:

- **Diversify across the major recommended sectors**
  - *11-13 healthcare stocks*
  - *9-11 financial stocks*
  - *9-11 technology stocks*
  - *5-7 energy stocks*
  - *3-6 stocks in other sectors with high safety rating*

- Select companies of a large size
  (5 billion market cap >)

- Select companies that possess a strong financial position as rated by Standard & Poors.

- Select companies that are No#1 or No#2 within their respective industry in; market share, debt levels, profitability, and FCF Yield.

- Select companies that have a P/E or P/S ratio below their 5-year average.

- Select companies that possess a PEG ratio less than 2 (for financial, healthcare, and energy stocks); less than 3 (for technology stocks).

The portfolio of 35 stocks that you maintain will be a balance of value and growth. Because the financial and energy sectors primarily contain value stocks, your overall average P/E ratio should be reasonably low. For a growth stock portfolio, maintain a P/E ratio below 22. For a value stock portfolio, maintain a P/E ratio below 15.

My recommendation is to immediately build a portfolio from the primary sectors. The principal emphasis should be industry leaders. Once your portfolio is built, just a little pruning will be necessary. You don't need to follow your companies like a hawk. Just ensure that you examine the fundamentals closely from time to time. Pay close attention to the P/E and P/Sales of your particular company. If the P/E or P/Sales climbs quite above the long-term average, then a good hard look at the firm's merits need to be examined. Watch for trends in the financial ratios discussed in Chapter 10. If the financial ratios deteriorate considerably, then selling your position is most likely warranted.

My primary buy strategy is to add stocks to the portfolio when those stocks in the recommended sectors are out of favor. In most circumstances, if a sector is out of favor, almost all of the underlying stocks will be out of favor as well. This is not always the case, but for the most part this rule applies. As we have previously detailed, the four major recommended sectors all possess low correlations. This means that generally one sector (or at least one sub-sector) will be out-of-favor at any given time. I generally sell when one or more of the following conditions are met;

- **Company failed to meet earnings expectations for two consecutive quarters.**

- **Company price/earnings (PE) ratio climbs well above the historical average.**

- **Financial ratios deteriorate.**

- **Free-cash flow yield drops below 4 percent**

- **Any accounting irregularities.**

In many instances, I will sell a stock holding if I believe the sector becomes extremely overvalued. This occurred in the technology sector in 2000. At the time, I simply could not find reasonably valued technology stocks. Additionally, there were several attractive stock candidates in the healthcare, financial, and food sectors. This turned out to be a prudent decision, as these sectors outperformed over the next two years. Presented below are five case study examples of my selection process. Each example covers a stock whose sector was out of favor at the time. These illustrations will give you a clearer picture of my recommended buy process.

CASE #1: ALBERTSONS
AUGUST 2000

My first case features a stock selection made outside the four traditional recommended sectors. For potential stock selections outside my favored sectors, I seek firms with strong defensive characteristics, high dividend yields, and a high safety rating by Value Line. During the first few months of 2000, the stock market was still at a remarkably high level. The technology sector had become extremely overvalued. I had reduced technology holdings to 10 percent of client portfolios, and increased exposure to healthcare to nearly 45 percent. The balance of the cash generally used for technology stocks went into other defensive sectors of the economy. I took a strong look at the food group, historically a group that performs well in troubled economic times. Supermarket companies were in dire straights. I began to focus on the three top firms within the sector; Kroger, Safeway, and Albertsons. Albertsons maintained both a high dividend yield and safety rating. As technology stocks boomed in 2000, Albertson's stock had an implosion. It commented that new store openings would be put on hold while the supermarket giant repositioned after reporting disappointing second-quarter earnings. Albertsons' stock adjusted itself too, plunging a stinging 33 percent to a new 52-week price low on Aug. 31, 2000.

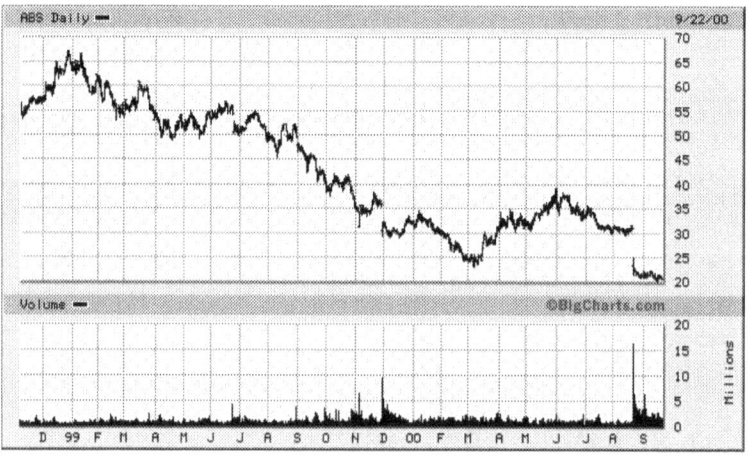

Table 11.1 Source: Bigcharts.com

CEO Peter Lynch (not the famous one) vowed to take the necessary steps to correct the operating issues, including establishing a renewed culture of thrift. Amazingly, Albertsons stock had been at $62 during December of 1998.

E.P.S.	$2.08
Current Ratio	1.3
Working Cap	905m
Debt/Equity	47%
Interest Cover	4.7
Operating Mrgn	7.7%
R.O.E.	15%
Price/Earnings	9.6
FCF Yield	22%

1. ABS was one of the largest retail food and drug chains in the United States. The company operated 2,512 stores in 36 states across the country.

2. ABS maintained a solid interest coverage ratio and a current ratio above 1. The company also maintained a single A investment grade rating from S&P.

3. Its P/E ratio was only 9. Historically, ABS had maintained an average P/E of 16 and a range of 10-23. Thus, ABS was trading at the lowest P/E ratio in the past 15 years.

4. If ABS could execute its merger successfully, potential earnings growth would be 10 percent through 2005.

5. ABS had the 2nd highest operating margins and R.O.E. within the large-cap supermarkets. Safeway was clearly the industry leader and had the highest margins. However it traded at a P/E of nearly 20. Safeway also did not pay a dividend. Therefore, I believed Albertsons offered the best value within the supermarket industry.

6. ABS paid out a 4 percent dividend per year and had a free cash-flow yield above 20 percent.

Albertson's stock rebounded throughout 2001, rising to $33 a share by the end of the year. I took profits in 2002 on Albertsons and placed the cash proceeds back into the technology sector.

CASE #2: NOKIA
SEPTEMBER 2002

In September of 2002, Nokia shares drifted lower after the number one mobile handset maker missed its key targets for profits growth in the second quarter. The company reduced its expectations for global handset unit sales to 400 million, which was at the bottom end of its earlier estimated range. Nokia's shares dropped an additional 7 percent to $12 a share, a price last reached in 1998. I had followed Nokia for the last several years, but felt the shares were always priced too high.

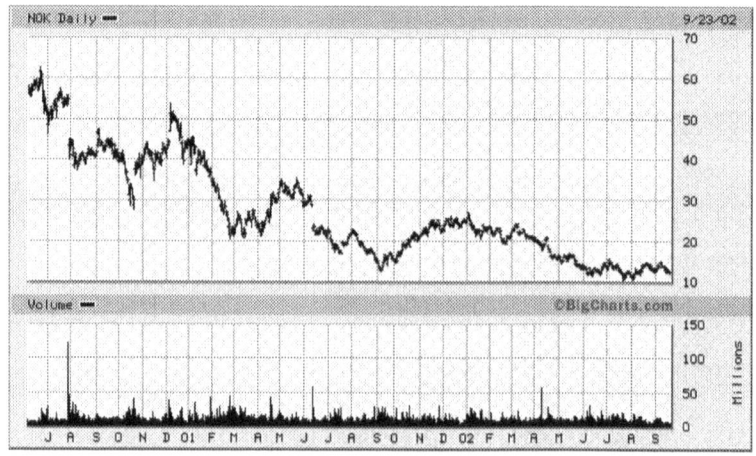

Table 11.2 Source: Bigcharts.com

At a current price of $12 a share, Nokia now offered an attractive entry point for technology investors. I first examined Nokia's financials;

E.P.S.	$.70
Current Ratio	1.8
Working Cap	8375m
Debt/Equity	2%
Interest Cover	212
Operating Mrgn	20%
R.O.E.	25%
Price/Earnings	18
FCF Yield	8%

1. Nokia was by far the leader within the cellular phone manufacturing industry.

2. Nokia had outstanding liquidity ratios and a minute amount of debt.

3. Despite the bedlam within the technology sector, operating margins actually rose during the previous year to 21.7 percent from 17.9 percent. The margins were far and above the best within their industry.

4. Nokia further reaffirmed its expectation to increase its market share lead in handsets in 2001. The firm had actually gained 2 percentage points in market share through the first six months of 2002.

5. Its P/E ratio of 18 was the lowest in almost a decade. The firm's historical P/E ratio range was from 16-85 over the preceding eight years.

6. The expected 5-year growth rate for Nokia was 15 percent. The PEG ratio was 1.2, extremely low for a premier technology company.

7. Nokia also met my criteria for FCF yield, at 8 percent.

I purchased Nokia one week later at an initial price of $12.35 As the NASDAQ stock market bottomed that October, Nokia had a tremendous run throughout 2003. I sold the firm's position in Nokia in early 2004 as it reached my price target of $20 a share.

CASE #3: TRANSOCEAN
NOVEMBER 2003

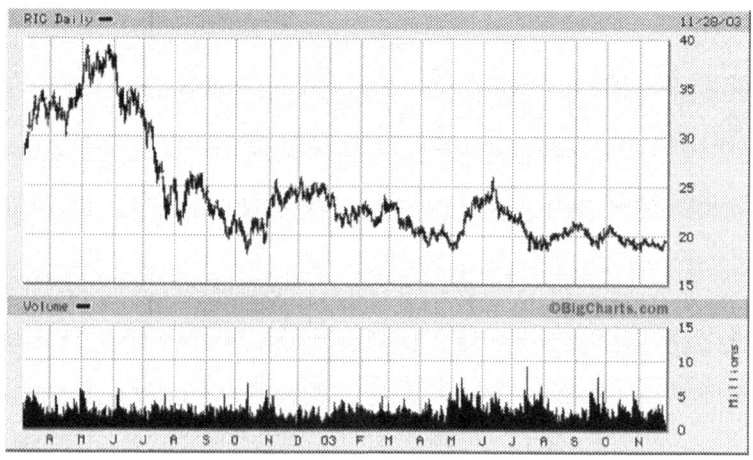

Table 11.3 Source: Bigcharts.com

Warm weather and fears of slowing growth led to severe trouble in the energy sector during 2003. During the latter half of 2002, oil and natural gas prices plunged to a two-year low. The price of light sweet crude fell below $25. Most energy analysts were very negative on the sector, predicting that the long-run oil price paradigm would continue to fall and the price would return to the $10 level of the late 1990s.

The combination of slackening demand and excess supply in the sector had a dramatic impact upon energy stocks. The energy sector, as measured by the Fidelity Energy Fund, fell over 20 percent during the 2001-2003 period. I screened the sector for investment candidates and unearthed Transocean, the leader in deep-water oil & gas drilling. Transocean was especially hard hit by the deep drop in oil and natural gas prices. Earnings per share at Transocean, which had climbed from $.67 in 2000 to $1.14 in 2002, fell to a low $.22 in 2003. Analysts were cutting their ratings and Transocean's stock price dropped 50 percent from a 2000 high of $65 (see table 11.4 above). At $20 a share, investors were discounting the worst in Transocean stock. I examined the fundamentals of Transocean in detail, starting with my favorite ratios pulled from the balance sheet and income statement;

E.P.S.	$.22
Current Ratio	2.34
Working Cap	6.3m
Debt/Equity	33%
Interest Cover	3.5
Operating Mrgn	31%
Net Mrgn	3%
Price/Sales	2.3
FCF Yield	10%

I concluded;

1. Transocean was an industry leader in the oil and natural gas exploration sector. The company had the highest operating and net margins within its industry.

2. Transocean had a strong management team led by industry veteran Robert Long.

3. Although Transocean had a relatively weak interest coverage ratio, the firm had solid cash flow and a reasonable current ratio. Therefore, I felt that the balance sheet could support further weakness within the oil and gas industry.

4. Despite a very poor 2003, Transocean still earned a positive E.P.S. of $.22 Due to the depressed earnings, I decided not to evaluate Transocean based upon a P/E ratio analysis. In this case, I relied upon the Price/Sales ratio. On a P/S basis, Transocean was trading at a 2.3 ratio. In the last 10 years, Transocean had an average P/S ratio of 4.9 Its P/S range, equally important, was 2.1 to 10.8 Therefore, on a relative basis, Transocean was trading near its historical trough level.

5. Transocean had an expected growth rate of 14 percent for the next five years. This was one of the highest growth rates in its industry.

6. Transocean had the largest fleet of rigs in the industry at 91. Day rates for these rigs were at a 10-year low. Since the industry was in a poor state, new rig construction was non-existent. Thus, if the deep drilling market returned to good health, new supply could not be brought to market quickly.

7. Transocean had a free-cash flow yield of 11 percent. Although earnings were low, cash flow was much higher due to the large amount of depreciation Transocean carried.

I felt that Transocean presented an excellent investment opportunity. Considering the price of Transocean had fallen so dramatically, I also felt the downside was limited due to the low P/S ratio. If the oil sector returned to favor, the potential upside was well above $40. Of course, it would take time for the investment to work. Investing in out-of-favor industries normally takes exceptional patience.

Fortunately, my need for patience with Transocean was minimal. Transocean's stock rebounded in early 2004, rocketing up to $43 a share by December of that year. This was a true homerun. As Transocean increased in price, I sold shares periodically to reduce the risk. Although this strategy capped the upside, it also protected me from Transocean's stock falling back to the original purchase price. As Joseph P. Kennedy once eloquently said; "Only a fool holds out for top dollar." Transocean continued to be an excellent performer. By summer of 2005, the stock approached $60 a share. At $60 a share, Transocean traded at a Price/Sales ratio of 5.5 This was still below the all-time high P/S ratio of 10.8. I continue to hold Transocean, believing it can reach $77 during the next two years.

CASE #4: SCHERING-PLOUGH
MAY 2004

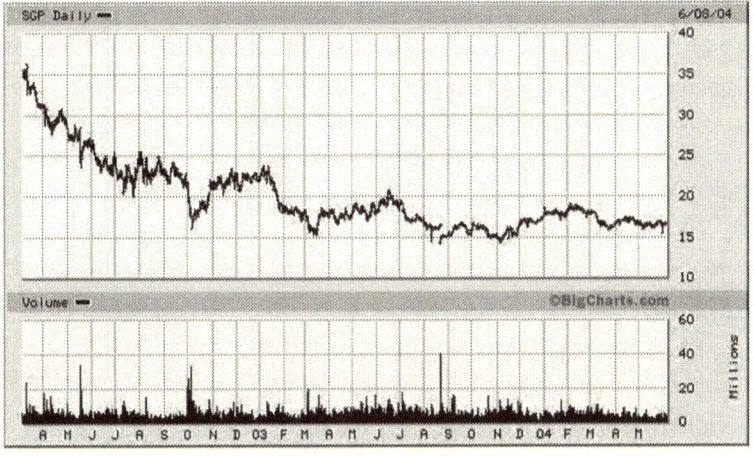

Table 11.4 Source: Bigcharts.com

Stocks in the pharmaceutical sub-sector were in the sick ward in 2004. Over the previous year, several large pharmaceutical companies such as Pfizer and Merck dramatically reduced earnings expectations. The AMEX pharmaceutical index had fallen from a high of $445 in 2001 to $312 by early 2004. Almost every pharmaceutical firm was out of favor with Wall Street. With healthcare being my top investment sector due to its extremely attractive profile of long-term return and future demographics, I was adding to the pharmaceutical sector throughout 2004.

My top target for a new stock addition was Schering Plough. Schering Plough was a more attractive company than many others in the industry. The company had lost most of its revenue two years earlier as Claritin was exposed to generic competition. With the loss of Claritin, total revenue started to decelerate, falling over 20 percent by early 2004. The stock also took a severe beating. It had fallen from a high of $61 a share in 2001, to a measly $17. I examined the fundamentals of SGP starting with a financial ratio analysis;

E.P.S.	$.25
Current Ratio	2.6
Working Cap	635m
Debt/Equity	22%
Interest Cover	7.4
Operating Mrgn	7.5%
R.O.E.	6%
Price/Sales	3.2

My analysis concluded;

1. Schering Plough had an excellent management team led by Fred Hassan. Mr. Hassan had been successful previously at Pharmacia where he led a turnaround of the beleaguered company. He was the perfect candidate to resuscitate SGP.

2. Schering Plough had solid liquidity and debt ratings. It had a low debt ratio (22 percent) in the sector that was rapidly improving since Mr. Hassan took over.

3. Schering Plough had a very low revenue base with terrific new drug prospects. Its newly launched drug, Vytorin, had already garnered 6 percent of the cholesterol market. Vytorin is expected to be a $6 billion dollar product by 2008.

4. With its pipeline of new drugs, SGP had the highest expected growth rate in the industry; 18 percent annual E.P.S. growth.

5. Schering Plough was trading at a P/S ratio of 3.2. This is one of the lowest P/S ratios within its industry. Its historical P/S range over the last ten years was 3.1 to 7.5. Thus, I felt safe purchasing SGP at its lower valuation range.

I purchased SGP for my clients at an average cost of $17.50 a share. In early 2006, Schering Plough was trading just above $20 a share. My 2007 price target for SGP is set at 5x sales, or $28.

CASE #5: J.P. MORGAN CHASE
OCTOBER 2005

In late summer of 2005, JP Morgan Chase's stock was caught in the banking sector downdraft. During 2005, the banking sector as measured by the S&P Banking Index had fallen from 375.59 to 332.68. This drop of nearly 15 percent was due to the Federal Reserve Bank raising interest rates. Higher interest rates, investors feared, would crimp the banks earnings as the spread between short-term and long-term rates converged. However, I felt that although interest rate spread profits would suffer, it was more than discounted in the stock price of J.P. Morgan Chase stock.

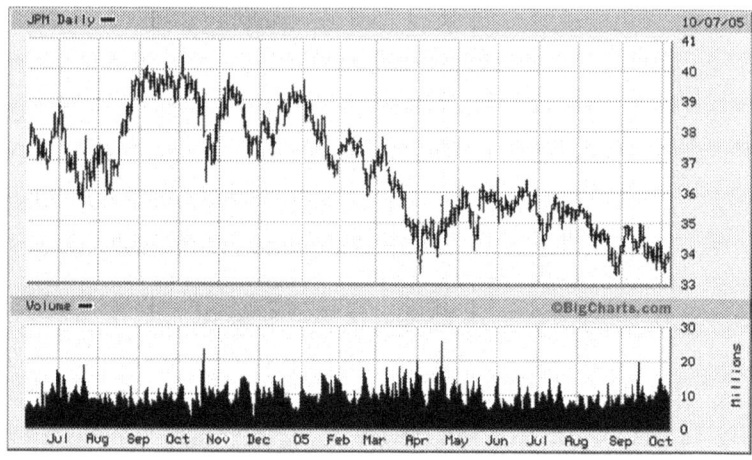

Table 11.2 Source: Bigcharts.com

I examined the financial ratios of the company;

E.P.S.	$2.90
Loans/Assets	33%
Interest Cover	2.04
Book Value	32.4
R.O.E.	11%
Price/Earnings	9.9
FCF Yield	11%

1. J.P. Morgan was a premier national bank.

2. Although the debt level was high and liquidity ratios low, it had the best ratios within its own industry.

3. The company's new president, James Dimon, would assume the role of chief executive at the start of 2006, six months earlier than planned. Mr. Dimon is considered one of the best CEO's in the banking industry.

4. J.P. Morgan Chase's P/E ratio was below 10. The historical range was 9-14. The average P/E over the past 10 years was 13.

5. The expected growth rate for JPM was 11 percent resulting in a PEG ratio of .9

6. It traded at only one times book value, a floor for most banking stocks. It traded at more than three times book value in the 1990's. I felt a reasonable expectation for JPM, with its new CEO leading the charge, was two times book value. That would result in a price target above $60 a share. I set this price target for mid-2007

I purchased J.P. Morgan Chase at $33.50 a share for our value accounts in 2005 and have continued to hold the shares. The stock broke the $40 price barrier in early 2006.

12

The Small Cap Hoax

"If a man dwells on the past, then he robs the present; but if a man ignores the past, he may rob the future. The seeds of our destiny are nurtured by the roots of our past."

—Master Po, Kung Fu Television Series

There are only two reasons to add an asset to your portfolio. Either you want it to reduce risk or you want it to add return. Hence the argument for investing in small-cap stocks. Affixing small-cap stocks to a portfolio of large-cap stocks has been thought to both add to performance and reduce overall risk (as measured by standard deviation). Small cap stocks have no doubt provided returns with a different performance pattern than large cap stocks. The true question for any investor is; do small-caps add long-term value to a portfolio?

To examine the merits of small-cap stocks, I must first define the term small-cap. Small-cap is a reference to market capitalization. Market capitalization is the number of shares outstanding multiplied by the share price. A company with a billion shares outstanding and a share price of $50 would have a market capitalization of $50 billion. This would be considered a large cap stock. A company with a million shares outstanding and a share price of $50 would have a market capitalization of $50 million. This would be considered a small cap stock. Note that in this example the price per share is the same. While it is true that small cap stocks often have a lower price per share than large cap stocks, it is not always true and the price per share has no bearing on the definition of a small cap stock. The definition of a small cap stock is not precise. I tend to utilize the $1 billion benchmark. Any company trading below this market capitalization is considered a small-cap. The line is drawn differently within the academic side of our business. Academic research suggests that small-caps are much smaller than a $1 billion to capture the desired effect. Academicians define small cap stocks as those companies whose market cap is in the smallest 20 percent of the total market cap for all companies. These smallest of the small-cap are sometimes referred to as micro-cap stocks.

And why is market capitalization important? Because history has shown us that the stocks of companies with different market caps behave differently in terms of return and risk. Several academic studies have concluded that over long periods of time, the stocks of small companies have outperformed those of large ones. They have returned more because small company stocks have a so-called risk premium. Therefore, the argument goes, because they are riskier you should be compensated by earning higher returns. Why more risk? Most small-cap companies are in the early years of their business evolution. And while they gain maturity, they have limited reserves against hard times. Also, if a smaller company loses a few key executives, or if the economy takes a turn for the worse, it only takes a few nervous investors to cause the stock to drop drastically.

Most financial planners and market commentators have recommended for years that small company shares be included in a diversified portfolio. They recommend this small-cap element due to their performance attributes and supposed risk reduction. I believe, however, that a small-cap hoax exists. Here are several of my arguments against investing in small-cap stocks including;

1. **Small-caps have substantial time periods of underperformance (especially in the last 20 years).**

2. **The 75-year small-cap return premium does not exist at all if six years of returns, 1977-1983, are exempted.**

3. **Institutions are now becoming more dominant in the capital markets.**

4. **Small-caps have a high level of downside risk and generally suffer most in bear markets.**

THE SIZE EFFECT

The "Small Firm Effect" is a market anomaly that has been documented by academics. In a widely promoted academic piece in the early 1980s, Rolf Banz published among the most important research papers regarding the so-called small firm effect *The Relationship Between Return and Market Value of Common Stocks* (Journal of Financial Economics, March 1981). In the study, Banz separated all New York Stock Exchange stocks into quinti zation (shares outstanding times stock price) and examined their returns. The average annual gain of the smallest firms was almost 20 percent higher than the largest firms. This small-firm effect spawned many subsequent papers that extended and clarified the early papers. In fact, a special issue of the *Journal of Financial Economics* was devoted to small-caps and contained several papers that extended the size effect literature.

The data presented in these studies has a few caveats. For six straight years, between 1976 and 1982, small-cap stocks (as measured by the Russell 2000 Index) had an average annual increase of 34.8 percent. This surge was primarily responsible for most of the academic articles showing that small-cap stocks have historically outperformed large cap stocks; 12.6 percent versus 10.7 percent since 1926. But when you take out this particular surge, small-caps have actually underperformed large-caps by almost 2 percent.

Period	Small Caps	Large Caps
1969-1974	-13.4%	3.4%
1984-1991	4.6%	13.7%
1995-1999	10.2%	18.3%

Table 12.1 Source: Russell Corporation

Since 1982, small-caps have lagged the market, earning 14.8 percent versus 16.2 percent for the large-cap index. Additionally, small-cap stocks have demonstrated several periods of underperformance (Table 12.1) In the five-year period ending in 1974, small-caps endured a substantial (16.8%) annualized return differential. During the seven-year period from 1984 to 1991, small-cap stocks returned a pedestrian 4.6 percent on an annual basis versus 13.7 percent for large-caps. From 1995 through the end of 1999 small-cap stocks returned an annualized 10.2 percent versus 18.3 percent for large-caps. Investing in small-cap stocks during one of these periods is akin to a driver hitting L.A. traffic, when momentum suddenly stops at rush-hour. You watch as your small-cap investments are slowed to a crawl. But the crawl is several years along before they finally can accelerate once again. This is the major risk to holding small-cap stocks; significant periods of inferior performance.

Other cracks have also appeared in the small-cap thesis. Several critics have pointed out that excess returns disappear after being consumed by small-company stock's fat transaction costs. Generally, the spreads between buy and sell prices of small-cap companies is higher due to the low volume. A Wharton professor once found that total trading costs for the buying and selling of the smallest stocks were sometimes more than 7 percent. In addition, many blue-chip advocates complain that Banz's database was just plain wrong. The standard academic stock-market database, Center for Research in Security Prices, fails to account for stocks that are delisted by stock exchanges for performance-related reasons. The CRSP simply ignores these stocks in its calculation, as opposed to hunting down their new, depressingly low price and computing their returns. As a result, I believe the CRSP overstates performance. Academic studies that have examined this phenomenon concluded that these NASDAQ delisted stocks could impact the long-term investment results of small-caps up to 3 percent.

THE IMPACT OF INSTITUTIONS

Small-cap stocks are also not popular with institutional investors. And this is problematic due to the fact that the institutional market is growing quite rapidly. It is becoming clear that these investors hold an ever-larger percentage of the country's equities, and simply put; large institutional investors prefer to buy large-cap stocks. Many pundits argue that the relative weakness of small-cap stocks since 1982 can be blamed on the growth of institutional investors, such as pensions and mutual funds. It is beginning to look as if it is having an effect. The evidence suggests that the growing power of institutions is having an adverse effect on the ability of smaller, sound companies to obtain investor recognition. Institutions have traditionally favored large-cap companies. This is due to the fact that many institutions have mandates on market limitations and risk concentrations.

Paul Gompers and Andrew Metrick[1], faculty research fellows at the National Bureau of Economic Research, arrived at that conclusion after correlating patterns traced by stocks and institutions. From disclosures statements, they found institutions managing at least $100 million of securities raised their percentage of the equity market from 26.8 percent in 1980 to 51.5 percent through 1996. They also found that during the same period, the 100 largest institutional investors grew in market share from 19 percent to 37 percent. Not only have these institutions come to own an ever-larger percentage of the country's equities, they also have a decided leaning toward the largest blue-

---

1.   "Institutional investors and equity prices," *Quarterly Journal of Economics,*
      116, 229-259. Gompers, P.A., and Metrick, A., 2001

chip stocks, which have become especially popular. The choice of large-caps has more to due with policy restrictions. Institutional investors are most often proscribed from owning more than 5 percent of a company's shares, a limitation easy to obey when investing in Microsoft. But this confines the institutions to only large, liquid stocks. A small company therefore rarely gets considered for investment simply because if a large fund purchased the shares, it would have an inordinate impact on the price of those shares. Plus, for the institution to take a large position, say 3 percent, they would have to take a large public stake in that small company. Together these phenomena add up to an increase in demand for large-cap stocks. And that increased demand helps explain the disappearance of any small-cap premium. Since the institutional market will only continue to gain prominence over the next decade, large-cap stocks will likely continue their ascendance.

DOWNSIDE RISK

Small-caps are inherently more volatile. Thus the chance of a dramatic loss from small-caps is higher than that of large-caps. When large caps declined in 1973 by 14.7 percent, small caps dropped 30.9 percent. In the crash of 1987, large caps dropped 30.7 percent but small caps went down 38.2 percent. The table below presents other down stock markets since 1985;

DOWN MARKETS: SMALL-CAP VERSUS LARGE-CAP *

	Small-Cap Decline (%)	Large-Cap Decline (%)
August 1987 to Oct. 1997	38.9	30.7
October 1989 to Oct. 1990	32.5	9.8
February 1992 to July 1992	12.2	1.9
May 1996 to August 1996	15.4	7.6

<u>DOWN MARKETS: SMALL-CAP VERSUS LARGE-CAP</u> (Continued)*

April 1998 to October 1998	36.5	14.8
March 2000 to Sept. 2002	39.1	41.5

 * *Table 12.2 Source: Ibottson*

As the previous table illustrates, with the exception of the 2000-02 bear market, large-cap stocks have suffered less during market pull-backs. Thus statistics indicate when a bear market occurs, small-cap stocks will bear the brunt of the decline. Avoiding large losses, as discussed earlier in this book, is a critical element in obtaining attractive long-term returns.

The general notion has always been that because small-caps possess higher risks, returns should inevitably be higher. This notion is non-sensical. Small-cap stocks have not outperformed large-cap stocks over the past 20 years. Data on the long-term returns of small-caps is also suspect. Perhaps small companies will outperform large-caps over the next 20 years, perhaps they won't. Due to the fact that small-cap stocks offer scant protection in bear markets, investing in small-caps is not worth the risk.

13

ETF's & Mutual Funds

"Only a fool holds out for top dollar"

—Joseph P. Kennedy

Unless you have at least $30,000 to invest, you should not invest directly in stocks. Instead, I recommend that you utilize funds to follow my investment strategy. The reason is simple; high costs. To be adequately diversified, you must own at least 35 stocks. Owning fewer stocks subjects you to additional risks for which you are generally not compensated. Owning less than 35 stocks will also prevent you from properly covering all the four recommended major sectors. The inherent problem with small accounts is that commissions and fees eat into your return. For example, say you attempt to maintain a 35 stock portfolio with only a $10,000 account.

To get your portfolio started (even if your account is held at a deep-discount broker such as Ameritrade), initial cost would be 35 stocks x $10.99 a trade, or $384.65. If turnover in the portfolio averaged 25 percent (or you sold and replaced a stock 7 times), additional commissions would amount to $153.86 Therefore, your total first-year trading costs would amount to $538.51, or 5.3 percent of your portfolio. Of course, after the first year, your trading fees would be reduced to 1.5 percent of your portfolio. However, that amount is still too dear. You should attempt to keep your trading costs less than 0.5 percent of your portfolio over time. So a $30,000 minimum requirement is quite prudent.

Once you have built up $30,000 in funds, you can begin to gravitate towards individual stocks. At the time you reach this dollar amount, it is fine to add to your portfolio one stock at a time. This is because you are still diversified by virtue of having most of your money in mutual funds. Merely limit yourself to investing no more than 3 percent of your money, to start, in any one stock. Gradually move out of funds and into stocks as time progresses.

ETFS

There are several different fund alternatives you can choose from including regular mutual funds, closed-end funds, and ETFs. ETFs are one of the most effective strategies. The acronym ETF stands for Exchange Traded Funds. Unbenounced to most investors, they've actually been around for years. As giant asset managers such as Barclays Global Investors and State Street have rolled out scores of new offerings in recent years, ETFs have once again gained the limelight. At the most basic level, ETFs are just what their name implies: baskets of securities that are traded, like individual stocks, on an exchange (most offerings currently trade on the American Stock Exchange). There are several advantages of ETFs;

1. *Trading Flexibility*—One key advantage that ETFs have over traditional mutual funds is trading flexibility. ETFs trade throughout the day, so you can buy and sell them when you want. Simply put, ETFs diversify an investment like funds but trade like stocks.

2. *Costs*—In terms of the annual expenses charged to investors, ETFs are considerably less expensive than the vast majority of mutual funds. Annual expense ratios for the largest ETF's (Ishares) range from 0.09 percent for iShares S&P 500 Index, to 0.99 percent for several of the iShares MSCI offerings.

3. *Taxes*—With a regular mutual fund, investor selling can force managers to sell stocks in order to meet redemptions, which can result in taxable capital-gains distributions being paid to shareholders. In contrast, most trading in ETFs takes place between shareholders, shielding the fund from any need to sell stocks to meet redemptions. Furthermore, redemptions made by large investors are paid in kind, again protecting shareholders from taxable events. All of this should make ETFs more tax-efficient than most mutual funds, and they may therefore hold a special attraction for investors in taxable accounts. Keep in mind, however, that ETFs can and do make capital-gains distributions, as they must still buy and sell stocks to adjust for changes to their underlying benchmarks.

4. *Performance*—ETFs are index funds. This means the fund owns a sampling of investments in its respective category, and does not try to select one company over another.

ETFs offer an excellent choice of investments. All my recommended sectors are available in ETF's. Four ETF investments offer global diversification, which I recommend;

S&P Global Healthcare Sector Fund (Symbol: IXJ)
S&P Global Financial Sector Fund (Symbol: IXG)
S&P Global Technology Sector Fund (Symbol: IXN)
S&P Global Energy Sector Fund (Symbol: IXC)

With four purchases, you can gain diversified exposure to all my sectors. In sum, ETFs are very low-cost investment products that deliver the diversification of mutual funds with the tradability of individual stocks. That is an exceptional package of qualities which explains why ETFs continue to grow in assets and breadth of product even through this bear market.

MUTUAL FUNDS

ETFs have several advantages over traditional mutual funds and offer a low-cost method to invest in the four recommended sectors. However, if you want to have an active manager select the stocks versus the index strategy that ETF's practice, there are several excellent alternatives within mutual fund families. Choosing a sector mutual fund in combination with ETFs can also provide enhanced diversification. There are two criteria you need to consider before choosing a mutual fund;

1. Never choose a mutual fund that has a sales charge, called a load, or one with a continuous load called a 12b-1 charge. These charges are detailed in the beginning of the prospectus that you must receive in order to invest in any fund. Academic studies have shown that there is no performance difference between a fund that charges a load and a no-load fund. A load is purely an additional cost that provides you no added benefit.

2. As with ETF's, choose a fund that has both a low expense ratio and low portfolio turnover rate.

I recommend the following active funds for each sector category;

Healthcare: Vanguard Health Care Fund (*Symbol:* VGHCX)

This is the best healthcare fund on the market today. With more than 18 years under his belt, manager Ed Owens has proved to be quite adept at choosing health care stocks. His fund continually ranks in the top percentage of healthcare funds. It's 18 percent annual return since 1992 is at the top of the list. The fund's volatility is also very low and its expense ratio is a minuscule 0.31 percent. Mr. Owens also follows a relative-value approach, choosing stocks in much the same manner as I recommend in Chapter 11.

Runner-Up: Fidelity Select Health Care (FSPHX)

Financials: T. Rowe Price Financial Fund (*Symbol:* PSIRX)

Over its eight year life, the fund has put up strong results. It consistently outperforms other funds within its category. Despite having three different managers during the stretch, the fund has consistently cranked out solid returns. Moreover, the fund has a deep bench with a solid cadre of junior analysts. The fund is well diversified across the different financials' sub-sectors and maintains a relatively small asset base (which allows flexibility). This financial fund typically holds companies with strong management, above-average earnings-growth rates, and strong market share. Turnover is also very low. The expense ratio, at 0.91 percent, is very reasonable and below the category average.

Runner-Up: John Hancock Financial Industries Fund (FIDIX)

Technology: Northern Technology Fund (*Symbol:* NTCHX)

Compared with its tech-fund peers, this fund has done an excellent job. It maintains a strong five-year track record, beating over 80 percent of its peers in total return. The fund is managed by John Leo and George Gilbert. Both are very experienced and have been with the fund since inception in 1996. Their portfolio is generally defensively positioned and concentrates on technology blue-chips. They tend to focus on buying companies with strong competitive positions that are gaining market share within their sub-sector. Large-cap companies are the primary focus. The expense ratio of the fund is a little high at 1.25 percent, but below the category average.

Runner-Up: Dreyfus Premier Technology Fund (DGVRX)

Energy: Vanguard Energy Fund (*Symbol:* VGENX)

Another Vanguard offering. This pure-energy fund maintains stakes throughout the energy sector, making it one of the most diversified funds available. The fund is led by longtime manager Ernst von Metzsch since 1984. Von Metzsch has a contrarian style, buying large-cap stocks that are out of favor. A sizeable portion of this energy fund is also earmarked for foreign stocks, giving it added diversification. Volatility is generally tame due to the fact that the fund maintains a high exposure to major oil companies. Being a Vanguard offering, its expense ratio is the lowest in the category, at 0.39 percent. With a sagacious investment strategy and low costs, this fund stands out among energy funds.

Runner-Up: Excelsior Energy & Nat Resources Fund (UMESX)

REIT'S & BOND FUNDS

Excellent alternatives within ETFs and mutual funds are also available for the recommended income components; real estate investment trusts, international bonds, and U.S. Treasury Bonds. Two ETFs I recommend include;

Cohen & Steers Realty Majors Index Fund (Symbol: ICF)
iShares Lehman 7-10 Year Treasury Bond Fund (Symbol: IEF)

There is currently no ETF for the international bond category. Therefore, I recommend the following mutual fund;

T. Rowe Price Intl. Bond Fund (*Symbol*: TRIPX)

This fund doesn't boast the best or most consistent performance record, but its primary attraction is the diversification benefits it provides. Most international-bond funds hedge their foreign-currency exposure so that their returns aren't affected by often-dramatic currency moves. This fund, however, keeps its currency exposure unhedged. Historically, unhedged funds have the lowest correlation with stocks. Its 22 percent positive return in 2002 bested all other funds within its category.

Runner-Up: Oppenheimer International Bond (OIBAX)

In the real estate and U.S. Treasury Bond categories, I recommend the following mutual funds;

Fidelity Real Estate Investment (*Symbol:* FRESX)

This fund has the largest assets in its respective category with a solid management team and low expense ratio. Manager Steve Buller prefers large, liquid companies and keeps the fund very diversified across all categories. This fund also tends to favor real-estate investment trusts (REITs) over real-estate operating companies (REOCs). It has been one of the top performing funds in its category over the last five years.

Runner-Up: Morgan Stanley US Real Estate Fund (MSUSX)

Strong Government Securities Fund (*Symbol:* STVSX)

The Strong Government Securities Fund is a slightly more aggressive than some other government bond offerings. This is due the fact that 10 percent of assets can be placed outside the government bond arena. But this fact has not resulted in any extra volatility or return deficiency. The fund has excellent long-term returns, although the expense ratio at .9 percent is high for a bond fund. The fund is also very consistent and has avoided finishing in its category's bottom in each of the last 10 calendar years.

Runner-Up: Vanguard GNMA Fund (VFIIX)

14

Avoiding The Bear Trap

"The further backward you look, the further ahead you can see."
—**Winston Churchill**

Avoiding a bear market is impossible. Bear markets are a component of investing. Every expert has a method to avoid bear markets. The most common technique is to utilize proper asset allocation. As described in Chapter 1, asset allocation involves allocating your money among different asset classes. Asset allocation is similar to diversification, but involves more strategy. Think of asset allocation as spreading your money across distinct investments and strategically allocating it among different asset classes. The goal of asset allocation is to obtain a proportional relationship among the various asset classes that will maximize returns and minimize risk, while taking into account your individual situation and goals. Proper asset allocation, according to most experts, will help you minimize the impact of a bear market.

The asset allocation theory (divvying up capital between various stocks, bonds and cash) dates back to 1952 when Harry Markowitz showed that an asset's risk was related to its volatility, but also it its correlation with other assets in the portfolio. The Markowitz model was the initial spark for academics to examine the relationship between different assets. Asset allocation gained national prominence after a landmark study conducted in 1986 by Gary P. Brinson, L. Randolph Hood and Gilbert L. Beebower.[1] The gentlemen found that 93.6 percent of the total variation in portfolio results was attributable to asset allocation. A follow-up study by Brinson, Beebower and Brian D. Singer[2] confirmed this result, indicating that asset allocation explained 91.5 percent of variation in returns. These results underscored the importance of a well-thought-out asset allocation strategy.

Through the 1990s, asset allocation garnered more and more attention. The theory also became more sophisticated. Instead of using just plain vanilla stocks and bonds, financial advisors started including sub-class categories, such as large-cap stocks, small-cap stocks, international and emerging markets stocks, corporate, government, and foreign bonds. Certain categories, like gold and real estate investments, were also included because they are considered by many to be separate asset class.

Now today, everyone is on the asset allocation bandwagon. This includes legions of financial planners, mutual fund companies, 401k sponsors, and the media. Asset allocation blueprints are now routinely published in major newspapers and magazines. The writers will profess how great these plans are and how they can help you secure a sound financial future. Business Week Magazine published a retirement guide back in July of 2000 and recommended three asset allocation plans based upon age;

1. *30-Year Old*; 60 % U.S. Large-Cap Stocks, 20% Small-Cap Stocks, and 20% International Stocks

2. *45-Year Old*; 45% U.S. Large-Cap Stocks, 25% Treasury Bonds, 15% Small-Cap Stocks, and 15% International Stocks.

3. *55-Year Old*; 50% Treasury Bonds, 30% Large-Cap Stocks, 10% Small-Cap Stocks, and 10% International Stocks.

---

1. Brinson, Hood, Beebower, 1986, "Determinants of Portfolio Preference", *Financial Analysts Journal*, 42(4), 39-4

2. Brinson, Singer and Beebower, "Determinants of Portfolio Performance II: An Update," *Financial Analysts Journal*, May/June, 1991

Most asset allocation plans are based upon age. The thinking goes like this; the younger you are, the more risk you can take with your investments. That's because you have more time to recover from market setbacks. If you're 30, you can afford to eschew bonds and concentrate mostly in stocks. As you age, the argument goes, preserving capital becomes more important. The Business Week article commented "By age 55, you'd be wise to put half your assets in bonds." Of course, at age 55, you may well live another 40 years and outlive your money. Your primary concern at age 55 should be maintaining growth in your portfolio to keep up with inflation. Protection of principal should be a secondary consideration.

There are several problems with the typical recommended financial plans that have been pointed out throughout this text:

• Bonds do reduce risk, but they also substantially reduce returns. Bonds have only provided a marginal return above inflation over the past 75 years.

• Small-cap stocks are not a well-founded investment choice.

• Adding international stocks can be beneficial for diversification. But only if the sectors added to the portfolio are different from the current sector weights within that portfolio.

Additionally, the aggressive recommended model portfolios (1 & 2) featured in Business Week did not protect you against a bear market. To prove this, let's examine these portfolios during the most recent bear market period, 2000-2002. Here are the results;

1. *30-Year Old Recommended Portfolio*
    2000 Return: -8.79 percent
    2001 Return: -10.71 percent
    2002 Return: -22.58 percent

2. *45-Year Old Recommended Portfolio*
  2000 Return: -3.08 percent
  2001 Return: -6.29 percent
  2002 Return: -14.58 percent

Both of the above portfolios suffer significant declines over the period. Let us examine the conservative third recommendation;

3. *55-Year Old Recommended Portfolio*
  2000 Return: 2.62 percent
  2001 Return: -1.68 percent
  2002 Return: -6.58 percent

Hallelujah! You've just figured out how to avoid a bear market. Well, not so fast. There is a downside to Business Week's model portfolio #3. You give up over 2 percent in annual returns compared against the S&P 500 stock index. Let's examine the long-term results of these 3 models;

Name	Return: 1976-2005
BW Portfolio #1	12.49%
BW Portfolio #2	11.03%
BW Portfolio #3	9.77%
S&P 500 Index	12.35%

Table 14.1

As you can see in table 14.1, the more bonds you add to the mix, the more depressed long-term investment returns become. Business Week's portfolio #1 did enhance return, albeit slightly, over the S&P 500 stock index, but its diversification did not impact the effect of a bear market on the portfolio. The returns for the period 2000-2002 are nearly identical for portfolio #1 and the S&P 500. Thus adding small-cap and international stocks did not help an investor sail through one of the most treacherous markets in history.

So, is there a model that outperforms the S&P 500, but can withstand the impact of a powerful bear market? Yes, there is. Listed below are two model portfolios based on the tenets of this book. I only recommend two model portfolios. This is due to the fact that either one of these models should meet your needs, whether you are 25 or 65 years of age.

Here are the 2 models and the characteristics of a comfortable owner;

1. Aggressive Portfolio (80% stocks, 20% bonds)

This portfolio maintains a high concentration in stocks. If you are below age 55 and can embrace a higher level of volatility, my aggressive model portfolio should be suitable for you. Conditions include:

- *high return expectations for your investments*

- *able to tolerate higher degrees of fluctuation (sharp, short-term volatility)*

- *are in the wealth accumulation stage of life*

- *have 10 years or more before you will need to utilize the money for your retirement*

Asset Allocation

32% Healthcare Stocks
12% Financial Stocks
12% Technology Stocks
8% Energy Stocks
8% Stocks in other sectors rated #1 for safety by Value Line
8% REITs

10% International Bonds
10% 5-Year Treasury Bonds

For those investors near or in retirement, then I recommend a balanced approach;

2. Balanced Portfolio (60% stocks, 40% bonds)

An intermediate risk portfolio that provides a blend of equities and income-oriented investments.

- *have moderate return expectations for your investments*

- *want some current income return on your investments*

- *are willing and able to accept a moderate level of risk and return*

- *are in retirement or approaching retirement*

- *are concerned about the impact of inflation eroding the value of your investments*

Now if you are a retiree, you might scoff at my recommendation of only 40 percent of your assets in bonds. In my mind, retirees have always put too much emphasis on bonds—ignoring stocks. This, too, can be a mistake. Remember that you could spend 20, 30, or more years in retirement, so you'll want stocks to help provide investment growth potential and hedge against inflation. This is especially true if you retire early, which many Americans are doing today. But even if you retire at the customary age of 65, statistics are still daunting. According to the census bureau, a 65 year old has a 40 percent change of living to age 90. If both a husband and wife are 65, there is almost an 80% chance one of you will live to age 90. And, that is not to say that you could not live to age 100. If so, that would be 30 years that your retirement portfolio would have to keep growing.

Therefore, you'll also want to maintain a diversified portfolio primarily based upon stocks. Here is the balanced portfolio recommendation;

Asset Allocation

24% Healthcare Stocks
9%   Financial Stocks
9%   Energy Stocks
5%   Technology Stocks
5%   Stocks in other sectors rated #1 for safety by Value Line
10% REIT's
25% U.S. Treasury Bonds
15% International Bonds

How do the two model portfolios stand up over the long-term? Actually quite well. The return on the aggressive portfolio, despite the 20 percent bond weighting, handily outperforms the S&P 500 Index. The balanced portfolio, despite its 40 percent bond weight, also outperforms the S&P 500 Index. The recommended portfolios also fair extremely well in bear markets. During the 29-year period (1976-2005), the aggressive portfolio only had two negative years (2001, 2002) versus the S&P 500's six (1977, 1981, 1990, 2000, 2001, 2002).

Name	Return: 1976-2005
Aggressive Portfolio	16.09%
Balanced Portfolio	14.25%
S&P 500 Index	12.35%

Table 14.2 Sources: (all tables within Chapter 14): Lipper Inc; A Reuters Company., 1976-2005. Financials measured by Financial Services Funds, Healthcare by Healthcare/Biotechnology funds (Comstock 1976-1981), Energy by Natural

Resources Funds, and Technology by Science and Technology Funds. REIT returns from the NAREIT index. International Bond returns from Roger Gibson. U.S. Treasury Bonds, Russell 2000, and EAFE returns from Ibbottson.

The drop in the aggressive portfolio during the most recent bear market was less than 5 percent. The S&P 500 dropped nearly 44 percent during this same three-year period. The recommended balanced portfolio, with its heavy weight in bonds faired even better. It gained nearly 14 percent from January 2000 to July 2005. Here are the annual returns for the S&P 500 Index and my two model portfolios;

YEAR	Aggressive	Balanced	S&P 500
1976	29.23%	24.88%	23.83%
1977	19.43%	16.87%	-6.98%
1978	10.56%	9.79%	6.51%
1979	35.18%	27.38%	18.52%
1980	47.90%	37.32%	31.74%
1981	4.30%	5.18%	-4.70%
1982	27.96%	25.73%	20.42%
1983	15.34%	13.18%	22.34%
1984	2.90%	4.84%	6.15%
1985	32.03%	29.27%	31.24%
1986	16.92%	18.02%	18.49%

YEAR	Aggressive	Balanced	S&P 500
1987	2.43%	5.10%	5.81%
1988	10.93%	9.52%	16.54%
1989	26.98%	21.93%	31.48%
1990	4.99%	5.95%	-3.06%
1991	45.06%	35.92%	30.23%
1992	8.52%	8.04%	7.49%
1993	12.35%	12.43%	9.97%
1994	0.83%	-0.45%	1.33%
1995	33.55%	28.21%	37.20%
1996	18.37%	15.12%	23.82%
1997	17.85%	13.98%	31.86%
1998	11.69%	9.37%	28.34%
1999	21.87%	12.52%	20.89%
2000	26.84%	23.60%	-9.03%
2001	-7.98%	-3.69%	-11.85%
2002	-10.67%	-3.89%	-23.96%
2003	30.58%	24.93%	28.80%
2004	13.04%	12.28%	10.88%
2005	9.68%	6.87%	4.83%
Annual Return	**16.09%**	**14.25%**	**12.35%**

Table 14.3

Here are my four recommended sectors and their annual returns since 1976;

YEAR	Healthcare	Financials	Energy	Tech
1976	39.62%	35.49%	21.37%	18.85%
1977	44.53%	-4.35%	-4.01%	0.10%
1978	9.37%	7.73%	11.96%	17.80%
1979	58.61%	16.62%	59.94%	29.47%
1980	90.58%	13.50%	52.02%	42.48%
1981	0.45%	16.33%	17.04%	-11.08%
1982	45.34%	18.66%	-10.81%	34.46%
1983	4.54%	26.42%	22.36%	34.25%
1984	-2.19%	15.76%	-10.78%	-10.13%
1985	44.61%	39.78%	15.15%	22.20%
1986	16.60%	15.13%	10.68%	6.44%
1987	-1.16%	-11.17%	9.18%	4.05%
1988	12.35%	19.26%	9.36%	4.87%
1989	46.33%	24.00%	34.31%	20.70%
1990	20.19%	-15.91%	-6.80%	0.87%
1991	68.41%	58.44%	1.35%	50.18%
1992	-6.65%	34.96%	1.48%	14.31%
1993	3.03%	15.67%	21.99%	25.58%
1994	2.62%	-2.68%	-2.92%	13.67%
1995	46.15%	41.88%	20.22%	42.52%
1996	13.07%	28.72%	34.42%	20.44%
1997	21.07%	45.82%	2.41%	10.21%

1998	18.83%	6.35%	-23.57%	52.04%
1999	19.13%	-1.26%	29.94%	134.22%
2000	55.10%	27.01%	28.15%	-32.91%
2001	-12.55%	-4.02%	-9.54%	-37.49%
2002	-18.85%	-10.87%	-6.25%	-38.82%
2003	32.51%	33.88%	33.40%	56.21%
2004	8.80%	13.91%	30.22%	4.05%
2005	9.33%	6.57%	41.11%	5.11%
Annual Return	**20.63%**	**16.02%**	**12.79%**	**13.77%**

Table 14.4

Here are the three income components and their annual returns:

YEAR	REIT's	International Bonds	Treasury Bonds
1976	39.15%	8.12%	15.98%
1977	18.04%	29.42%	1.29%
1978	9.43%	18.50%	-0.78%
1979	33.23%	-4.99%	0.67%
1980	29.65%	13.69%	-2.99%
1981	6.14%	-4.61%	8.20%
1982	28.27%	11.89%	32.81%
1983	29.55%	4.33%	3.20%
1984	21.85%	-1.97%	13.73%
1985	11.85%	35.01%	25.71%

1986	24.79%	31.35%	24.28%
1987	-6.13%	35.15%	-4.96%
1988	14.52%	2.34%	8.22%
1989	6.73%	-3.43%	17.69%
1990	-15.97%	15.29%	6.24%
1991	40.28%	16.24%	15.00%
1992	28.30%	4.77%	9.36%
1993	15.46%	15.12%	14.21%
1994	-8.39%	5.98%	-8.04%
1995	12.07%	19.55%	23.48%
1996	33.84%	4.08%	1.43%
1997	19.37%	-4.26%	9.94%
1998	-15.38%	17.79%	14.92%
1999	-1.98%	-5.07%	-8.25%
2000	28.38%	-2.63%	16.66%
2001	13.17%	-3.54%	5.57%
2002	4.07%	19.54%	14.16%
2003	24.53%	18.98%	5.65%
2004	32.24%	11.41%	5.22%
2005	11.75%	-9.54%	3.59%
	REIT's	**International Bonds**	**Treasury Bonds**
Annual Return	**15.36%**	**10.28%**	**9.55%**

Table 14.5

Notice the strong performance of the three recommended income ingredients during the most recent bear market (2000-2002). Each category had a positive three-year return, offsetting the losses of the stock component. During 2002, when the four recommended stock sectors fell by an average 20 percent, the income component truly saved the day. International bonds had almost a 20 percent gain due to a weak U.S. dollar. U.S. Treasury Bonds also performed well as interest rates fell. Many investors would have given up on international bonds after three consecutive years of declines (1999-2001). But when you needed this category to step up to the plate and help your portfolio during 2002, it did. This is one of the key elements of a successful investment strategy. Develop it, implement it, and most importantly, maintain it through thick and thin.

The implication of these results is that typical asset allocation is counterproductive. In an attempt to lower risk and garner superior returns, pundits add small-cap and international stocks. Small-caps do not add value. International stocks only add value when a portfolio is sector balanced. As the Business Week model returns demonstrated, adding these two asset classes had no significant impact on either long-term investment returns or bear markets. In fact, the only method to avoid a bear market within traditional asset allocation is to add bonds. This does limit the impact of a bear market and decrease the portfolio's long-term volatility. However, since the bonds with low short-term volatility also have sub-par long-term returns, the process of classic asset allocation will only dilute an investor's gains. In my mind, these arcane models are a waste of time. Only by examining the markets in a different light, sectors, can you attempt to secure true diversification.

The sector strategy promoted in this book gives you the opportunity for outstanding investment returns with less risk. Instead of simply investing in the S&P 500, you are siphoning out the best performers. The four sectors, healthcare, financials, energy, and technology all possess excellent long-term results with low correlations. Combined with my favored income component suggestions (REIT's, international bonds, and U.S. Treasury Bonds), these sectors are the true path to a high return, low risk portfolio. Most importantly, when a bear market appears, you will be more than ready to ride out the storm.

About the Author

Timothy J. McIntosh is the CEO of Strategic Investment Partners LLC. Mr. McIntosh holds a Bachelor of Science Degree in Economics from Florida State University. He has also attained a Master of Business Administration (MBA) degree from the University of Sarasota and a Master of Public Health Degree (MPH) from the University of South Florida. He is a Certified Financial Planner (CFP) and a CFA Level II Candidate.

Mr. McIntosh has served as an adjunct finance professor at Eckerd College since 1998. He has been featured in the *Wall Street Journal, New York Times, USA Today, Fortune, Barrons, and the St. Petersburg Times.* He has recently been named one of the top 150 financial advisors in the country for doctors by *Medical Economics Magazine.* He and his wife, Kim, have two sons and reside in Tampa, Florida.

.

Glossary

American Stock Exchange (AMEX). Second largest stock exchange in the United States. First known as the Curb Exchange because it started on the streets of New York City.

Balance Sheet. The summary of a company's assets, liabilities, and shareholders' equity. Since balance sheets do not list items at their current monetary value, they may overstate or understate the real value of certain corporate assets and liabilities. Also called the statement of financial condition.

Bear Market. A declining stock market that is 20 percent from the highest price level

Beta. This measures the volatility of a share of stock. A high beta stock, for example, will rise more in value than the stock market average on a day when shares in general are rising. And it will fall more sharply than the average on a day when shares are falling. The Standard & Poor's 500 Index of stocks, an index that represents large-company stocks, has

Big Board. Name for New York Stock Exchange

Blue Chip. Large, financially strong corporations with little investment risk, and good records of earnings and dividend payments.

Bond. A corporation's I.O.U. note. The issuing company usually promises to pay bondholders a specific interest for a certain length of time and repays the loan on the expiration date. A bondholder is a creditor of the corporation and not a part owner. as is a shareholder.

Book Value. Book Value is often used as an indicator for selecting undervalued stocks. It is also used to determine the ultimate value of securities in a liquidation. Book value is calculated by the following: Total assets minus intangible assets (goodwill, patents etc) minus any long-term liabilities EQUALS total net assets. This figure, divided by the number of shares of preferred and/or common stock, gives the Net Asset Value—or Book Value—per share of preferred or common stock.

Broker. An agent who handles the public's orders to buy and sell securities. There's a commission for this service.

Bull Market. An advancing stock market.

Capital Gain or Capital Loss. Profit or loss from selling securities.

Certificate of Deposit (CD). A money-market instrument with a set date of maturity and interest rate issued by banks.

Commission. The broker's basic fee for purchasing or selling securities.

Commercial Paper. Debt instruments by companies to meet short-term financing needs.

Common Stock. Securities that represent an ownership interest in a corporation.

Correlation. The simultaneous change in value of two numerically valued random variables: *i.e. the positive correlation between cigarette* *smoking and the incidence of lung cancer; the negative correlation between age and normal vision.*

Depression. Economic period with high unemployment and business failures.

Debt to Equity Ratio. A measurement of financial leverage—the use of borrowed money to enhance the return on owner's equity. It is calculated by Long-Term Debt divided by Common Stockholders Equity. The higher the ratio, the greater the leverage and risk.

Dividend. A payment to stockholders from the corporation's earnings On preferred shares. it is usually fixed. On common shares the dividend varies with the prosperity and needs of the company.

Dollar Cost Averaging: A system of buying securities at regular intervals with a fixed dollar amount. Under this system the investor buys by the dollars' worth rather than by the number of shares. If each investment is at the same number of dollars, payments buy more when the price is low and fewer when it rises. Thus temporary downswings in price benefit the investor if he continues periodic purchased in both good times and bad and the price at which the shares are sold is more than their average cost.

Dow Jones Industrial Average. This is the best known U.S. index of stocks. It contains 30 stocks that trade on the New York Stock Exchange. The Dow, as it is called, is a barometer of how shares of the largest U.S. companies are performing.

Earnings. A term generalized term referring to corporate profits. Profits can be calculated in different ways depending upon the industry and accounting practices. Earnings is one of the frequently used measures of a company's financial condition. It is commonly used to determine the risk/reward profile of a given security—the ratio of stock price to earnings (see P/E Ratio).

Earnings per Share. The dollars of profit generated for each share of common stock. A company that earned $1 million last year and has 1 million shares outstanding would report earnings per share of $1.00. The figure is calculated after paying taxes, preferred shareholders and bond holders.

Equity. Ownership of common and preferred stock

Federal Reserve Banks. Twelve banks created by the Federal Reserve Act. The banks serve as agents for the U S government and its monetary policy.

Growth Stocks. Stock of a corporation that has exhibited faster-than-average gains in earnings over the last few years and is expected to continue to show high levels of profit growth. Over the long run, growth stocks tend to outperform slower-growing stocks but they also tend to have higher price/earnings ratios, lower or non-existent dividends, and are consequently, riskier investments.

Individual Retirement Account (IRA). A self-funded retirement plan that can be made through mutual funds. insurance companies and banks or directly in stocks and bonds through stockbrokers. Employed individuals can contribute up to a maximum yearly sum while deferring tax on interest until retirement.

Inflation. A fall in the value of money and a rise in prices.

Insider Information. Important facts about plans or condition of a corporation that have not been released to {he public.

International Bonds. Bonds that are issued in a country by a non-U.S. entity. International bonds include eurobonds, foreign government bonds, and global bonds.

Load. The portion of the offering price of shares of open-end investment companies in excess of the value of the underlying assets which covers sales commissions and all other costs of distribution. This load is incurred only on purchase in most cases. It is known as a front load. If there is a load upon selling it is called a back load.

Liquidity. Ability of the market to absorb a reasonable amount of buying or selling with reasonable price changes

Margin: The amount paid by the customer when he uses his broker's credit to buy a security. Under Federal Reserve regulations, the initial margine required in the past years has ranged from 50 percent of the purchase price all the way to 100%.

Money Market Funds. Mutual funds that invest in the shortest money market such as commercial paper CDs and Treasury bills.

Mutual Fund. An investment company that sells shares of itself lo the public and invests the money in securities. Gives individuals opportunity to take less risk through a diversified investment.

NASDAQ. National Association of Securities Dealers automated quotations system is an electronic stock market. Provides brokers and dealers With price quotations on securities traded over the counter.

Net Change. Change in the price of a security from the closing price on one day to the closing price on the next trading day.

New York Stock Exchange (NYSE). World's largest securities market. Only stocks in major corporations that have met the exchange's requirements for financial solidity are listed

Over the Counter. Market conducted by phone and mainly with stocks not listed on an exchange, Dealers act as principals or as brokers for customers.

PEG. A valuation measure which compares the P/E ratio of a company to its earnings growth rate (Price/Earnings to Growth, hence PEG). The P/E and earnings growth rates used can be either trailing numbers or forward estimates.

Preferred Stock. Stock with a claim on the company's earnings before payment can be made on common stock and usually entitled to priority over common stock if the company liquidates.

Price Earnings Ratio (P/E Ratio). Price per share of stock divided by earnings per share for a 12-month period. A popular way to compare different priced stocks. For example. a stock selling for $30 per share and earnings of $3 a share would be selling at a PE ratio of 10

Price to Book Value. Also called Multiple to Book Value, it is a measure of the relative risk/reward profile of a stock. It is calculated by dividing the latest stock price per share by the most recent per share value of stockholders equity (book value). A company with a stock price of $12 per share and a book value of $6 per share is trading at two times book value. Generally, the higher the multiple to book value, the riskier the stock is, however, it is important to know that multiples vary from industry to industry and should be considered as such

Recession. Mild decline in economic activity with a decline in employment and trade.

REIT. Real Estate Investment Trusts are publicly traded companies that manage portfolios of real estate to generate profits. The underlying assets are investments in shopping centers, medical facilities, office buildings apartment complexes, hotels, and various other real estate holdings. One type of REIT takes equity positions in real estate and distribute the income from rents and capital gains (when properties are sold) to shareholders. Other REITs act as lenders to property developers and pass interest income on to shareholders. A third type of REIT combines equity and mortgage investments. To avoid taxation, REITs must distribute 95% of their taxable income to shareholders annually.

Return on assets. A useful indicator of how profitable a company is relative to its total assets. Calculated by dividing a company's annual earnings by its total assets, ROA is displayed as a percentage. Sometimes this is referred to as return on investment.

Return on equity. This is a company's net worth divided by net income. Investors use ROE, as it is called, as a measure of how a company is using its money.

Russell 2000 Index. A market capitalization weighted index published by Frank Russell of Tacoma Washington, the Russell 2000 is one of the most widely regarded measures of the stock price performance of small companies. It is a part of the Russell 3000 Index consists of the 3000 largest U.S. stocks in terms of market capitalization. The highest-ranking 1000 stocks are in the Russell 1000 Index (which closely mirrors the S&P % Index). The remaining 2000 stocks, the Russell 2000 Index, represent approximately 11% of the Russell 3000 Index's total market capitalization.

Sector. A common way to group a broad array of companies that are in the same line of business. Within a sector you can have many industries. And each industry consists of well-defined industry groups. For example, Technology is a sector. Internet is an industry subset of Technology, and Internet Service Providers is a specific industry group within the Internet category.

S.E.C. The Securities and Exchange Commission created by Congress to help protect investors by regulating stock transactions.

S&P 500 Stock Index. Standard and Poor's index of 500 widely held stocks, representing about 70 percent of total market value of American stocks.

Standard Deviation. A measure of the dispersion of a set of data from its mean. The more the difference from the mean, the higher the standard deviation. In finance, standard deviation is applied to the annual rate of return of an investment to measure the investment's volatility (risk). The more volatile the stock, the higher the standard deviation.

Take-Over: The acquiring of one corporation by another—usually in a friendly merger but sometimes marked by a "proxy fight."

Top-down approach. A method of security selection that starts with analyzing the economic conditions, then developing asset allocation for a portfolio. It then works systematically through sector and industry allocation to individual security selection.

Value Stock. A stock that trades at a low valuation versus its earnings and sales. Trades at a low P/E ratio and generally pays a generous dividend.

U.S. Treasury bill. U.S. government debt with a maturity that is less than a year is a bill.

U.S. Treasury bond. U.S. government debt with a maturity of more than 10 years is a bond.

U.S. Treasury note. U.S. government debt with a maturity of one to 10 years is a note.

Volume. Number of shares traded in a security or an entire market for a given period. usually considered on a daily basis.

Wall Street. Street location in New York City—one of the major financial centers of the United States.

Yield. Also called return. Yield is the dividends divided by market price of the stock expressed as a percentage. A stock with current market value of $50 with a dividend of $2.50 has a yield of 5 percent.

Index

978-0-595-27224-2
0-595-27224-X